Vocal and Stage Essentials for the Aspiring Female R&B Singer

Vocal and Stage Essentials
for the Aspiring Female R&B Singer

A GUIDE TO TECHNIQUE, PERFORMANCE, AND MUSICIANSHIP

Terri Brinegar

Hal Leonard Books

An Imprint of Hal Leonard Corporation

Published in 2012 by Hal Leonard Books
An Imprint of Hal Leonard Corporation
7777 West Bluemound Road
Milwaukee, WI 53213

Trade Book Division Editorial Offices
33 Plymouth St., Montclair, NJ 07042

Diagram of the human voice/vocal cords (p. 7) © Maryna Melnyk/Dreamstime.com
Images of piano keyboard (pp. 15 and 45) © John Woodcock/iStockphoto.com

CD piano accompaniment by Jamey Whiting
CD vocals by Terri Brinegar
Inside photography by Robert Sadler

Printed in the United States of America

Book design by Leslie Goldman/Wild Cherry Studio Inc.

Library of Congress Cataloging-in-Publication Data
Brinegar, Terri.
Vocal and stage essentials for the aspiring female R&B singer : a guide to technique, performance, and musicianship / Terri Brinegar
p. cm.
Includes bibliographical references and index.
ISBN 978-1-4584-1653-7
1. Singing–Instruction and study 2. Rhythm and blues music–instruction and study. I. Title
MT820.B856 2012
783'.0643143–dc23

www.halleonardbooks.com

contents

preface

I remember the exact first moment that I heard the blues. I had just moved to Los Angeles and was living in a room-for-rent with a shared bathroom down the hall and a hot plate and mini-fridge (sounds like the blues already). I could hear everything that went on in the room next to mine, and my neighbor was a blues fan. He played blues songs day in and day out. Something struck me in an odd and beautiful way that day, and I couldn't shake the feeling. It hasn't left me since.

I also remember a feeling of panic when I first tried to sing the blues. Coming straight from a serious classical background, I was afraid I would sound like Mary Poppins singing the blues. It took *years* of listening, studying, and practicing to feel comfortable enough to get onstage and try out what I'd learned. *That* was intimidating, but through trials and tribulations I've learned a lot. And I would like to share what I've learned with younger people who may be discovering this music for the first time or who may not understand the importance of this music to our heritage and culture as Americans.

I find it interesting that I have a love for (what may be described as) black music: blues, soul, gospel, and R&B. Not only am I a white, middle-class, middle-aged woman, I am from a family of bluegrass musicians. My parents and older sister formed a band when I was a child, so I was surrounded by bluegrass and country music from a young age. We had musicians (some of whom are now famous) over to our house to jam quite often. Every summer we would go to bluegrass music festivals and camp out. I loved waking up to the smell of bacon frying, the sounds of banjos and guitars being picked, and singers harmonizing during early-morning jam sessions. My dad is a music historian of sorts and has always encouraged me to explore my "roots." My family played traditionally "white" music—music that had its origins in Europe, which formed one part of our American musical tradition. Another component of that musical tradition came from involuntary settlers, the African slaves. And for some reason black music is where I have found my musical passion. I have always wanted to explore this musical heritage in depth; to know and thoroughly understand the roots of R&B and the influence of the music of the slaves, spirituals, and the blues, and how these musical genres have been transformed into R&B and hip-hop. This musical journey has intrigued me, and, considering my background, my own fascination with it has baffled me. The first record I purchased was Rick James' "Mary Jane"—go figure!

One reason I wanted to write about this music is that I don't think most American youths understand the importance of this heritage to the American musical tradition as a whole. In fact, music of black origin has affected many aspects of American music: blues, soul, R&B, rock 'n' roll, and jazz. I want young people of all backgrounds and ethnicities to understand where we come from, what our roots are, and the significance of seeing something that was once painful and tragic (slavery) transformed into something beautiful and magical. I want to help young people understand the power they hold in their voices, in their words, in their musical expression, in expressing who they are. I believe music *can* transform the world—and it has!

acknowledgments

I would like to thank all of my students; you have helped me to learn so much!

I would like to thank my wonderful husband, Jim, for all his love and support. He always believes in me.

introduction

I'm writing this guide for several reasons: I am a professional singer with a classical background; I teach singers how to sing "properly" and apply that "proper" technique to any style of music. Because I have education in classical music as well as performing experience in the blues and R&B world, I have a unique approach to singing. I've learned it, I've applied it, and it works! I'm now in my forties and I am still singing high Cs and performing professionally.

Many students come to me after working with "contemporary voice" teachers, teachers who teach country and rock 'n' roll music. My approach is to teach technique first, then focus on the genres.

I've been teaching for a long time. I teach everyday singers, the average person who wants to sing for enjoyment, the good singers who want to become great . . . all styles, all ages, all levels of accomplishment. I get to teach not only classical, but rock, R&B, jazz, blues, Broadway, pop, and country. And because I've taught such a varied group of individuals, I've learned a huge amount! I could not have learned what I've learned if I had been teaching only opera students with exceptional voices. Trying to convey technique to those who have never before studied voice has forced me to dig deep. The more I teach, the more I learn.

I now see singing as a spiritual thing, very simple yet very complex. I've come up with about a thousand analogies (*think this, think that*) because the voice is buried deep within the body. You can't even see your vocal cords; even a doctor has to use special instruments and mirrors to actually see the voice working. I now seem to know, on an intuitive level, what the student needs.

It's not just about technique, but *technique is the first step*. A lot of students resist classical technique at first, because they are afraid they'll sound like an opera singer, when they want to sound raspy like Janis Joplin. But technique is the foundation of proper vocal production. The musical style in which you use it is your choice. With a good, solid foundation of technique, you can sing any style and have range and flexibility. Why limit yourself?

And besides, you are born with the voice you are born with! You shouldn't try to force your voice to sound like someone else's. Be who you are and make the most of it. Your voice is special and unique. Find your own sound, find what works for you, sing in the range you are meant to sing in, find songs that work with your voice. It may take time, but once you find all of that, you will have personal *style*. And that's a very important thing to have!

OVERVIEW

The Book

The book is divided into five sections: Vocal Technique, Rhythm & Blues, Musicianship, Performing, and The Basics.

Each heading is followed by a discussion of that particular topic, and then a section titled "How to Do It" presents clear, concise instructions on how to achieve that particular technique.

It also includes two CDs: Vocal Warm-up Exercises and R&B Exercises, with written-out (transcribed) notation and explanations of all of the exercises.

The CDs

The Vocal Warm-up CD (CD #1) has my vocals performing every exercise with piano accompaniment on Tracks #1–15. Start with this CD and sing along with me until you are comfortable with the exercises. Tracks #16–30 are the piano accompaniment alone. These vocal exercises work for any style of singing, from beginning opera to contemporary R&B and pop. (Vocal technique will be discussed in detail in Section 1 of this book.)

Most of the exercises start at G (below middle C) and proceed by half-steps to high C. Some of the exercises are for specific purposes; for example, they may work the break area (which I will explain in detail later). Those exercises only include that range of the voice, not the entire scale. Start and end on the note that is comfortable for you; don't feel like you have to do the entire two and a half octaves. Everyone's voice range is different, so just do what works for you. Use different scales on different days, so you can use a variety of exercises to work different areas of your voice. Mix it up!

I sang the exercises myself, with just live voice and piano. This just shows that my technique works! I've never lost my voice or missed a gig. I sang the vocal warm-up exercises using the "classical" technique, because I believe this is the foundation of singing, just as you would study classical technique if you studied piano or dance. You don't have to sing them with as much vibrato as I do—that's my personal style—but use the other techniques, which I will describe in more detail later in the book.

The R&B CD (CD #2) starts with the minor pentatonic scale (Track #1), then continues with several examples of "riffs" (Tracks #2–26). I sing three different versions of each riff, using different vocal effects to show the versatility of each one. There are two songs/grooves in which I sing several of the riffs (Tracks #27 & 29), followed by the piano accompaniment for you to practice with (Tracks #28 & 30).

vocal technique

BEFORE YOU SING A NOTE

I'm going to teach you the basics of good vocal technique and how to sing "properly," regardless of what style of music you're going to sing—so let's get started!

Keep It Simple!

I tell students, if you only had to think of two things in singing (and there are a million things to think of), think *open and open*—open your mouth and the back of the throat to have good resonance, and open the rib cage to ensure good breath support. You have to boil it down to the basic elements, especially when you're onstage performing. In front of an audience you want to focus on the song and expression of it, not the technique—this should come naturally by that point. So keep it simple and get to the core. *Keep it open!*

Analogies

Because your voice is literally buried in your body, I have to use analogies to get you to "visualize" how to sing and to "see" the notes. I'm going to be saying, "Think this" and "Think that." With other musical instruments, you can see the keys or the strings and frets, and a teacher can show you where to move your fingers or how to strum. But with singing, your body is your instrument, so I must get you to think about the functions of your muscles in order to sing properly.

Practicing

How much should you practice? How often and for how long? Think of it as starting a workout regimen at the gym: you want to start slowly and work your way up. So start at about twenty minutes per day, four times a week. Then slowly work your way up to forty-five minutes to an hour, several times a week.

But before you sing anything, stretch your body. Release any tension you may be holding in the shoulders, neck, and throat by rolling the head and shoulders. Then stretch your voice by doing some slow yawns and sighs from high to low. Let the note just float down; start easy and let your voice get ready for singing. Feel that light, high whistle-tone at the high end of your voice. Don't use any pressure, just float it.

When you start vocalizing, start with medium volume, not full volume. Your body is your instrument and you must treat it with gentle care. The sigh-down will help to get your voice and body in proper shape before actually singing, opening your throat and gently massaging your vocal cords. Remember to keep it light. You can also sing a gentle sigh-down, going down the scale in half steps and gliding down to the bottom, about two octaves. (We will discuss all of the vocal exercises in detail at the end of the book.)

Posture

Make sure you use proper posture, straight and aligned, when singing. Keep your chest high, but keep your neck and shoulders relaxed. Don't put your weight on one foot or the other; stand evenly, your weight centered evenly over both feet. Keep your hands out of your pockets, so you won't have the tendency to slump, and keep your chin parallel with the floor (don't tilt your head back or look down). And please, please don't practice in your car! Cars have "bucket" seats, designed for comfort, not for singing. There's no way you can have good breath support while sitting in a bucket seat. You need to have a straight back when singing, so standing is important for good support. Sitting while singing, especially in the car, is not recommended!

THE VOICE

The human body is a miracle: it can create sound. It can then create breath pressure to move that sound across the room. Sound is created by air moving between the vocal cords. It's possible to force the vocal cords together with brute strength, but you don't want to do that; you want to use air. Just as you can create sound by blowing air between two pieces of paper (try it), you can create sound by "blowing" air between your two vocal cords. It's the same concept: air passing between things that vibrate can create sound.

The vocal cords move close together for high notes and farther apart for low notes, and the air passes between them. If you look at the photo, you will see the open space between the cords when we breathe. To vibrate the cords, there must be air pressure, which comes from the breath in your lungs. Other areas of the head, such as the tongue, cheeks, lips, and palate, can affect the sound and strengthen or weaken it. The trachea is the passageway for the air and includes the larynx, which encases the vocal cords.

7

Location of the vocal cords

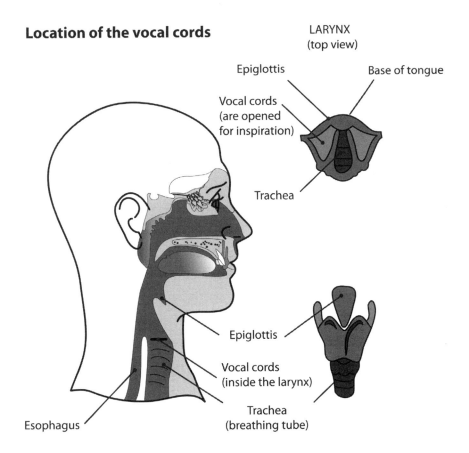

Figure 1.1. The human voice.

BREATH

Breath is the foundation of life: you can't survive without it. You can't sing without it, either. Good breath technique can make or break your voice; it affects every part of your singing: pitch, dynamics, tone, timbre, and phrasing.

Diaphragmatic and Abdominal Breathing

I don't know how many times I've heard my students say, "My choir teacher said to sing with my diaphragm." I want to shoot the first choral director who came up with that! To this day I cannot find with complete certainty the exact location of my diaphragm muscle! How can I use it if I can't even find it? Diaphragmatic breathing may be the "correct" term for this type of breathing, but it's very confusing, since we cannot actually locate this muscle in our bodies and feel it moving. All I know is, it moves up and down and is essential for breathing.

Diaphragmatic breathing is considered "deep breathing," because your breath goes down into your abdomen, deeper than just chest breathing. It is used often in yoga to attain deep relaxation, among other things. The diaphragm is a dome-shaped muscle that moves down and flattens out when you inhale, and returns to its dome shape when exhaling. It does this automatically; even when you're sleeping, it's working. But as singers, we have to control our breath. It's easy to take a big gulp of air inward, but we also have to control our exhalation; that's the hard part!

So when I exhale, I can feel my abdominal muscles pushing the air out as they move (from bellybutton to spine) inward. I'm not trying to push my breath up or down, so it's very confusing to think of the diaphragm. But I can feel and identify my abdominal muscles and can control them one hundred percent. I can control the amount of air that leaves my lungs in direct correlation to the amount I push my abdominals in. Stomach in, breath out. Simple! It's like a balloon: you squeeze the balloon and the air pushes out.

Sound is created by the breath moving over the vocal cords, not by forcing the throat muscles to work. Yes, you can actually create sound without any breath at all by forcing the muscles together, but you want to use breath, not brute strength, to create sound. Remember, the throat is just a passageway for the breath to move through; it should be easy. The real work happens in the body, from the bottom of the neck down to the belly button.

Think about a ballet dancer: she may seem so graceful on stage. It looks easy, right? But you know her body is using serious muscle strength, even with the seemingly simplest movement. And all the while, her hands are graceful and relaxed. Do that with your singing: let your body have serious muscle strength while your throat is relaxed. Separate your body into two parts: the throat (the gateway), and the body (the strength and support system). Simple, right?

Well, it's really not so simple. There's really no other thing, sport, or exercise that uses the same type of breath technique as this (except for maybe yoga or swimming). So it's hard to compare it to anything else.

Flexible Tension

I mentioned that the body creates breath pressure. *This* is the most important aspect of singing in my opinion. It's easy to breathe in; anybody can gulp in a big breath. But exhaling in a controlled fashion, applying even pressure to every note . . . that takes work.

Think about a bellows—oh, you might not know what that is! It's an old-fashioned device used to fan a fire; it has two handles, and you push them together to push air into the flames. The air exits from a long, narrow spout, just like your mouth! If you were to install a spring between the two handles, there would have to be pressure to push the air out, similar to the pressure needed to push the air out of your lungs.

How do we create pressure in our own bodies? There must be resistance. You can't resist if there's nothing to resist against. Confusing? Think about two opposing magnets; they resist against each other. You can almost see the pressure between them when you try to push them together. You are pushing them together and they are pushing out, resisting each other. Now think of the muscles in your back and rib cage pushing out, resisting the impulse to collapse. You keep your body open in your back and use your abdominal muscles to create the pressure. If your rib cage collapses, there's no way to create pressure.

Here are some other ways to think about it: how about a big, thick rubber band? When you pull and stretch it out, it takes resistance to keep it there. What about a spring door? It takes resistance to keep it open when what it naturally wants to do is slam shut. You have to resist against that force by pulling the door open to keep it open. I call this "flexible tension." You want resistance without being too tense. Think of your rib cage like a big rubber band: you must expand it and use resistance to keep

9

it open; otherwise it will snap shut! Keep it open, but not too tense, and not too loose, either. Try not to let the rib cage collapse. (The Three Bears theory: not too little, not too much, but *just* right.) It takes years of practice to find that perfect amount. Easier said than done!

Breath vs. Breath Pressure

To create more breath pressure, you just use more air, right? Wrong! Using more breath pressure doesn't necessarily mean more breath; it means putting more resistance in the body, more strength in the abdominal and back muscles, working together. More pressure does not necessarily mean *louder;* it means more pressure to focus the sound through. Finding the right amount of pressure takes a lot of practice, and we'll talk more about this technique in the sections that follow. You will find that you need more breath pressure for the more demanding songs or genres, like classical, and less for soft rock, for example. In any genre, you will start to notice a change in your tone and greater pitch accuracy once you start to use correct breath pressure.

Open the Rib Cage

Inhale slowly through the nose, feeling your rib cage expand all the way around, as if you are a barrel expanding. Your stomach will come out a little, your ribs will expand horizontally, your back will even come out a little. Exhale through your mouth, using either a buzzing of the lips or blowing with pressure like through a straw. Now, when you exhale, don't let your body collapse! How can you create pressure if there's nothing to resist against? Use your abdominal muscles to do the work of exhaling. Notice that the amount of pressure your abdominals use is directly proportional to the amount of pressure exiting your mouth.

If you start to run out of breath, move your shoulders back. That will open up the space in the rib cage and will tighten the back muscles. You want to feel the muscles in the back holding on. It won't be comfortable at first, but you'll get used to it. The back muscles are what are holding the rib cage open. The spine is the center of your body; the muscles attached to the spine are the center of your breath, so to speak. Those muscles must be used! I recommend using a stretchy belt or Ace bandage wrapped tightly around your midsection, so you become consciously aware of your breath. Try to keep your rib cage as open as possible. Yes, it will collapse some, but you don't want it to just collapse immediately like a balloon releasing air and flying off. You want to gradually apply pressure to the abdominals while keeping the rib cage as open as possible. Once the rib cage collapses, it's all over; now there's no way to create pressure. (Remember, you want the breath to create the sound, not the throat muscles.)

Meanwhile, you don't want your body to become concave when you're running out of breath. Instead, move the shoulders back, feel those back muscles engage. Ever wonder why people slump when they walk or sit? Because it takes *effort* to keep the back muscles engaged. It's not comfortable or natural in reality. Your body wants to move with the force of gravity and fall to the ground in a fetal position. To keep it from doing that, you have to use the *back muscles*. In time, your muscles will develop more strength and the work will come naturally. It will feel good to expand your rib cage and keep the back muscles taut. You'll be using your body to sing, not just your throat. Your body is your instrument!

Now try holding a note, using that same breath pressure. See the note moving across the room like a laser beam: strong and focused, reaching its destination, not fizzling out or fading away, but strong until the last second of the note is sung. If you start to run out of breath, move the shoulders back and think "crescendo," or "louder," to move more air through. You have more air than you know, and there is a little reserve air in your lungs. Use those back muscles, use those abdominal muscles, open the rib cage, and think "out" as your ribs start to move inward. (Think of the abdominal muscles as the "control center" as they move in and out and control the flow of breath. Think of your back as a "constant" that stays as open as possible.)

Water Hose Analogy

If you've ever watered the lawn with a water hose, then you know about breath pressure. Here's why: when you water the lawn, you turn on the water full blast to get the water to move to the far side of the lawn, right? What if you had only a trickle of water? You'd have to turn up the *pressure* in order to move the water across the yard. So it is when you're singing soft notes (with less breath): you must turn up the pressure to move the notes across the room, as well as to have the necessary breath required for good pitch, vibrato, and tone. You create pressure by opening up the rib cage and using those abdominal muscles, with strength, to move the note across the room.

Nose Breath vs. Gasp Breath

It's easier to take a big breath through the nose, because you can increase the breath little by little. So when there's time in the music, take a slow nose breath. However, you can still get a full breath, even if there's not much time in the song to take a nose breath. If you are leaving your rib cage open, then when you have to take a quick gasp breath, you won't have so far to go. You won't have to completely fill up the lungs and expand, because you'll already be expanded. So you'll be able fill up with a lot of air quickly. A gasp breath will also raise the soft palate, which helps the pitch and resonance.

how to do it

Inhale slowly, expanding the rib cage and back muscles.

Expand all the way around your body, like a barrel.

Exhale, either pursing your lips together or buzzing (like a motorboat), with pressure from your abdominal muscles.

Pace yourself as you exhale, not releasing all the air at once.

Keep your back muscles open (think *out*!).

Use your abdominal muscles to control the breath as you exhale, feeling the correlation between the pressure from your abdominal muscles and the amount of pressure in your breath.

Use the strength in your body to create breath pressure, not the throat muscles.

Use even pressure for every note, from the first note to the last.

Walk around with a full breath, keeping your head, neck, shoulders, and jaw relaxed.

Exhale slowly.

Do some dog panting, and feel your abdominal muscles doing the work of pushing the air out.

Figure 1.2. Relaxed (before inhaling), ribs are collapsed.

Figure 1.3. Full breath, ribs are expanded.

Figure 1.4. Relaxed (before inhaling), ribs are collapsed.

Figure 1.5. Full breath, ribs are expanded.

14

RANGE

Sing in the range that's comfortable for you. Too many singers try to emulate their favorite singers and force their voices to sing notes that are not even in their range. Don't do that! Know your range; know your capabilities. The main melody of the song should be in the middle part of your range, so there's room to hit a few high notes and sing a few low notes. You don't want the whole song too high or too low. Just because you like the sound of a song on the radio doesn't mean it works for you—find the key that does. If you have to manipulate a track or chart to transpose it into your key, then do that. Our voices are all different; celebrate the uniqueness of yours!

The typical voice range is about an octave and a half. If you have a two-octave range, than you're doing great! (A three- (or more) octave range is not so common, and is usually typical of highly trained singers or highly gifted natural voices.)

Here are the typical ranges of voices:

Soprano: C4–C6

Mezzo-soprano: A3–A5

Contralto: F3–F5

Tenor: C3–C5

Baritone: F2–F4

Bass: E2–E4 (some basses can sing low C2)

Figure 1.6. Middle C.

how to do it

Know your range, where your high and low notes are.

Try to sing melodies that are in the middle of your range so you have 3 or so notes on either side of your high and low notes.

Transpose songs if necessary.

RESONANCE AND TONE

You are born with your voice; it's not as easy to change its tone as it is to change the tone of an electric guitar. With a guitar you simply turn the knobs; your voice cannot be so easily manipulated.

Nevertheless, it can be changed! You can learn to sing with big, open space to get a fuller tone. As you increase the volume on an amp, it can also affect the tone (ask any guitarist). The more energy sent through the amp, the fuller the tone. More energy (breath pressure) will give you a fuller vocal tone (another reason breath is so important). Less breath pressure will give you a weak-sounding tone, and nobody wants that! Just remember to apply breath pressure from the abdominal muscles, not from the throat!

Resonating Cavities

Your head has several resonating cavities, which can change your tone and enhance your overall sound. There's lots of open space in your head! So use it to your advantage. The more space you have, the more resonance. Think about a guitar or violin: the bigger the space, the deeper the tone, right? Have you ever seen one of those big Mexican bass guitars? Deep tone and huge sound!

How about a piccolo—teeny amount of space, and teeny, high-pitched sound. Nobody I know wants a teeny voice; everyone wants big sound, full resonance. In order to do that, you must have *space*! You have open space in your mouth, the back of your throat (pharynx), and your nasal cavity. There's not much you can do about the dimensions of your nasal cavity, but there's a *lot* you can do about your mouth and pharynx to create and maintain space.

Mouth

I want you to get in the habit of singing with a long, narrow, open jaw. Later we'll do some vowel exercises to work on this, but for now, just think *long* and *narrow*. It's easy to let the jaw shut at the end of phrases, so you have to focus on it. Look in the mirror; you may think your mouth is open, but is it *fully* open? Have you ever seen a famous singer on TV who's singing with his or her mouth barely open? Never! They always have big, open mouths, no matter what word or musical phrase they are singing, however high or low.

Space is very important to good tone. You must open up, but be relaxed, too; don't force the jaw open or hold tension in the jaw, because that's not being relaxed. Form the shape of a yawn, nice and open and relaxed. Think that your mouth is in an oval shape from top to bottom and the tongue is relaxed against the bottom teeth. You don't want your tongue tense or bunched up. A little smile in the cheeks helps to keep the pitch lifted (I call it "Joker Face").

Pharynx

The pharynx is an area at the back of the throat behind the mouth. It actually has several parts to it, but we'll be focusing on the parts we can actually control. Like I said earlier, you want space to create great resonance. The only way we can control the pharynx and the space available there is by lifting the soft palate (the area at the back of the roof of the mouth).

When you yawn, your soft palate lifts automatically, which creates big space in the back of your throat. You can't go around yawning before you sing a phrase, now, can you? But you can *think* big space; imagine there's the space the size of a ping-pong ball at the back of your throat. If you smile while you sing, you can even lift the soft palate a bit. A gasp breath will also raise the soft palate and create space.

how to do it

Drop your jaw, mouth long and narrow in a relaxed way like a yawn.

Lift your soft palate (think the space of a yawn).

Keep your tongue relaxed against bottom teeth.

Have a little smile (Joker Face) in the cheeks to keep the palate lifted.

Figure 1.7. Right! Long and narrow jaw; lots of space between roof of mouth and jaw; flat tongue.

Figure 1.8. Wrong! Spread wide; no space between roof of mouth and jaw.

PITCH

Support the Note

Breath support definitely affects pitch: think of a small plastic ball in a vertical tube you can blow into to keep the ball suspended in the air. As soon as the air subsides, the ball drops down. It's the same thing with the breath: if your breath support falters, so can the note. You want to think even and steady with the breath support, so the note is not falling into musical potholes! Also, imagine you're riding the upper side of the note. That note has many dimensions to it, and we're not computers singing exactly in tune all the time. Singing on the upper side of the note does not necessarily make it sharp; it just makes it lifted. If the note is dragging, it will sound dull and blah, but singing on the upper side makes it bright. Visualize that you are riding on a magic carpet, floating on the note.

Singing Descending Notes

Some students think that descending a scale is easier than ascending. They think the climb is difficult, that the high note is the peak, and that the descent is easy. Not so! As you descend the scale, you must not let the breath support falter. If you are climbing down a mountain, it takes just as much effort, or more, to get down the mountain as it did to get up it, right? You have to have steady footing or you could slip and fall. So must you have steady breath as you descend, or the note will slip and fall. Think that as you descend, you're taking one step at a time and that every step is supported underneath.

Notes That Jump

When jumping down from higher notes to lower notes, visualize that you are jumping onto a solid surface, not a trampoline! You don't want the note to go "boing" as it scoops down and back up. You want the note to land squarely on pitch, so it must be supported as it jumps down. You have to control the breath pressure.

Hitting High Notes

Have you ever seen a glass elevator? As you watch the elevator ascend, you can see all the cables fall down to the bottom. As one goes up, the other comes down. Well, that's the analogy for hitting the high notes: you are not reaching up for the note; you are just opening up the space at the top and thinking *down* as you ascend. It's like one big yawn, with big space in the back of the throat.

Imagine that the throat is that glass elevator; as the note goes up, the space in the throat drops down and opens up. Too many students close up the top trying to hit the high notes, when they should do just the opposite: relax and let the note out with gentle pressure. The note doesn't need to be forced or cajoled out of the throat—it wants to soar and be sung! Relax the back of the throat, think down and open up. You're not trying to squeeze out the note; it's already there, and you want to just allow it out! (In actuality, you are keeping your larynx lowered, which is very important for proper technique.)

Here's another analogy: think of a train loaded up with bricks going up a hill. It gets bogged down as it climbs higher and higher, and it needs more energy (coal) to give it the push needed to make it up the hill. Now think of your voice, weighted down with big notes; it also needs extra energy (breath) to help get it up the hill. The breath is the energy that can lift the note to where it needs to be. (Also note that high notes require more breath pressure than lower notes.)

how to do it

Keep your cheeks lifted as you sing; it will keep the pitch slightly lifted.

Visualize riding on the upper side of the note.

Keep the breath support even and steady (keep the back muscles engaged); don't relax as you descend.

Think down as you ascend.

Let the note out naturally, no pushing or squeezing.

Open up with the space of a yawn and relax the back of the throat.

Use more breath pressure as you ascend

PHRASING

When you yawn, the jaw drops, the tongue relaxes against the bottom teeth, the soft palate lifts, the rib cage opens up, and the lungs gradually fill with air. It's all a very relaxing process, right? However, so many students will breathe in the air in this relaxed manner, but when they exhale the throat closes up and they get stiff in their bodies and throats. Often when a phrase begins with a word starting in a vowel, a student will do what's called a "glottal stop," where the vocal cords actually come together and temporarily close off the breath.

You can feel this in your throat: the muscles are working to create the sound, rather than allowing the breath to do that work. For a brief moment, you are actually choking off your breath, like squeezing the neck of a balloon. (Remember, we want to create the sound with our breath, not by forcing our throat muscles together. Think "reverse yawn.")

Let me explain: start the note in the same position as a yawn, and exhale. That is, keep your jaw dropped, tongue relaxed, throat open, soft palate lifted, and breath relaxed and steady. Nothing should change in the throat between inhaling and exhaling; only the direction of the air changes and sound is put to it. It should remain relaxed and open, just as in a yawn. Don't choke yourself just because you want to sing a note. That makes no sense! Keep it all open and relaxed. You may want to put a little "ha" at the beginning of those words starting on vowels to make sure the breath is flowing, and that you're not starting with a glottal stop.

Now think about the note actually moving across the room, or in an arc, in a phrase of music. It has a destination, a beginning, and end. It needs to go from Point A to Point B, and you want all the notes to receive equal attention. You certainly don't want the notes at the end of the phrase to fizzle out or splatter against the walls. You want the notes moving in a steady, narrow stream, as if you were singing through a paper towel roll. In order to do this, you must keep the breath pressure moving forward; never retract the breath. Think about it moving forward; see it!

If you start to run out of breath at the end of the phrase, *crescendo*! Get louder in order to maintain the breath pressure. Don't let those last few notes wither away; they all deserve the same amount of attention. There must always be a continuous flow of energy into the note, keeping it moving forward. Move your shoulders back if you start to run out of air; there's a little pocket of air left, just enough to sing the last notes fully. See the note with a little propeller on the back of it, moving it forward at a steady pace.

20

Songs vs. Exercises

When you first start learning a song, even if it's in English, you may want to drop the words and sing on an *Ah* so that you can concentrate on the *two main elements* of *open and open*. *Ah* is the sound you make when the doctor says, "Open up and say *Ah*!" That's the *Ah* I'm talking about: big and open.

You may want (at first) to think of the song as an exercise: a series of scales, jumps, ascending and descending lines. Use the same principles as you do in your warm-ups: keep the jaw long and narrow, and the rib cage open. Focus on your phrasing, focus on pitch, apply dynamics. Once you have the basic elements of the song, then you can add the words.

how to do it

Think "reverse yawn"—keep the throat open, jaw dropped, tongue relaxed, rib cage open.

Start with a small "ha" so the breath starts flowing.

Move the shoulders back to engage the back muscles when running out of breath.

21

SINGING VOWELS

We do vowel exercises to learn how to sing all the vowels long and open. Remember, you want the jaw dropped; your mouth should be in an oval shape, with as much space as possible between the jaw and roof of your mouth, long and narrow. Exercise #9 below will help with the five main vowels: *Ah, Eh, Ee, Oh,* and *Oo*. We learn to sing all those vowels in the shape of "ah," to the best of our ability.

Let's get to the basics and focus on *Ah, Eh, Ee, Oh, Oo*. These five vowels are "Italian" vowels, since in Italian they are sung in a pure form and are always nice and big and open! Our English equivalents of these vowels are:

Ah (as in *a*ll, n*i*ght, b*o*dy)
Eh (as in b*e*d, p*e*n, or s*e*t)
Ee (as *ea*sy, bab*y*)
Oh (as in R*o*man, *o*ld)
Oo (as in bea*u*tiful, t*oo*l, *u*sed)

Figure 1.9. Right! Lips are puckered for the *Ee*, space is visible between the teeth.

Figure 1.10. Wrong! Mouth is spread for *Ee*, no space, teeth biting down.

We're going to split the vowels into two parts: *Ah, Eh, Ee* and *Ah, Oh, Oo. Ah* is the largest and most open of the vowels, and in each sequence the space becomes smaller, either from the jaw closing or from the lips coming together. We want to try to maintain as much space in the mouth as possible, regardless of which vowel you are singing, in order to have consistent tone.

In *Ah, Eh, Ee* your jaw and tongue lift up to form the vowels. So you have to learn to keep your jaw as long as possible and not let your mouth close down or spread wide (as in a smile). It's pretty easy to keep the *Eh* long, but not so easy with the *Ee*. You actually have to pucker in order to keep space between the roof of the mouth and jaw on the *Ee* vowel.

With *Ah, Oh, Oo,* your lips come together to form the vowels. So you don't actually have to close your mouth in order to say these vowels. Just move your lips closer together, while trying to maintain the space between the roof of the mouth and the jaw.

But what about the other vowels, the "ugly" vowels, like *Uh* as in "love," *Ih* as in "it," or *A* as in "cat"? None of those vowels sound pretty, nor are they very open. So we have to modify these vowels into the shape of the five main vowels. You know how to sing those five vowels open, right? So now think one of those vowels when singing an "ugly" vowel. For instance, when singing "love," think *Ah.* It won't sound like "lauv"; it will still sound like "love," but it will be open and have good tone and resonance. When singing "cat," think *Ah;* it will sound like "cat" but be open.

And then there are the diphthongs: vowels that are actually two vowels in one. ("I" is actually *Ah* plus *Ee.*) In these cases, stay on the most open part of the vowel the longest when singing; don't let it go to the *Ee* until the very last second. That way you'll maintain the open space for the longest time while singing. Another example: the word "stay" is actually *Eh* plus *Ee;* stay on the *Eh* the longest, then go to the *Ee* at the very end of the note.

Consonants should be sung quickly, with a quick snap, then straight back to the vowel. Remember, vowels carry the sound, consonants cut it off. You want to have a smooth and connected (legato) flow of the sound.

23

how to do it

Learn how to sing the five main vowels as open as possible (Exercise #9): *Ah, Eh, Ee, Oh,* and *Oo.*

Modify other vowels into the shape of the five main vowels.

With diphthongs, stay on the most open part of the vowel the longest.

Always think long and narrow, no matter what vowel you are singing.

Don't change the shape of the vowel just because you add words.

Keep the same vocal tone, regardless of which vowel you are singing.

PLACEMENT

The difference between sounding like an opera singer and sounding like an R&B singer has a lot to do with placement. Placement is where the sound is resonating in your mouth. In opera, the back of the throat is very important for achieving a huge tone and is very open. However, you can have an open throat while still moving your placement from front to back. In R&B, you want to incorporate that space at the back of the throat while keeping more of a forward placement.

In your head, there are several resonating cavities: the nasal cavity (can't do much about the size of that one); the mouth (open long and narrow with as much space as possible between the roof of the mouth and the jaw); and the pharynx, which is the back of the throat (lift your soft palate as in a yawn, and feel that space open in the back.). Try it: say *Ah*, then think it in your nose, think it in the back of your throat, think it on your teeth. Overexaggerate it so you really hear the tone change.

The "classical" tone would be more of a back placement, an *Aww* sound; an R&B tone would be more of a front placement, as in *A* or *Eh*. You have the power to move your placement around and change your tone, just like a guitarist adjusts the knobs on his guitar and amp. Slight variations in the shape of your mouth can have a huge impact on your tone. Always think long and narrow and open, because you always want a *big* sound regardless of the tonal quality of the sound.

Here's another analogy: think of a concert hall, with a lot of space from the roof to the floor, as well as space in the wings on the side of the stage. Now, where are you going to stand to perform there? Right up on the edge of the stage, in the wings, in the back of the stage, or right in the center? Of course, you want to be right in the center! Would the sound change if you moved to the back of the stage or to the wings? Of course it would. So think of your mouth as a mini concert hall. You want it open with lots of space, and you want to have your tone centered. Think of your note as a shiny disco ball hanging from the center of the ceiling—there's your placement.

how to do it

Sing *Ah* and try to move the placement from front to back and back to front.

Really get a feel for the different tones you can create depending on where you are centering the sound.

Stay centered, incorporating all the open space in your head.

VOCAL BREAKS

We all have breaks in our voice, some more noticeable than others. Some of my favorite singers have no noticeable break; they just flow from high to low and back again very naturally and easily (yes, I know . . . I'm jealous, too!) There are registers in a voice that let us sing only so high before we have to switch to the next register. These are called chest voice (the lower register), and head voice (the higher register).

Just as a stick-shift car can only go so fast before it needs to change gears, the voice can only go so high before it must change gears. In a stick-shift car, you put in the clutch to ease the pressure on the engine momentarily and move into the next gear. In singing, you ease the pressure of the breath momentarily . . . and switch gears! You must lighten up on the breath pressure for just a moment while moving into the next register or you will *crack*! It's the breath pressure that makes a voice crack, or trying to push the voice up too far in range.

Sing in the range that's comfortable for you; don't try to push up too high! I'm not a fan of "belting" your voice (pushing it high with the chest voice). I believe wherever the natural break is, is where you should change gears. (Too many voices have been strained by trying to force the voice into a range where it should not be!) Know your range; know where your break is.

There is a middle ground, an area where you can sing in either head or chest voice. It is usually the weakest part of the voice and tends to be smack-dab in the middle of the voice for female singers. Practice singing in this range in both head voice and chest voice. Once it is stronger, then you can choose to sing in head or chest depending on what the music dictates and the phrasing. How does it sound to stay in one register; how does it sound and feel to switch? You want a good blend between chest and head for a smooth transition.

25

how to do it

Know where the break is in your range.

Practice Exercise #11 for break area strength.

Ease up on your breath pressure to transition between registers.

VIBRATO

It has been my experience that vibrato comes naturally once the breath support kicks in. The vocal cords need that steady breath pressure to get them to vibrate. Some teachers have students do little exercises, similar to trills, in which they alternate between notes that are close together to simulate vibrato. But really, it's not a musical/vocal thing; it's a breath pressure thing. I can turn vibrato off and on, and I feel it in my abdominal muscles. When I use more breath pressure, I feel my stomach muscles push in more. So it seems to me that vibrato is really controlled by the breath pressure—the more you have control of your breath pressure, the more you'll have control of your vibrato.

I personally think that vibrato is something acquired through regular practice of proper breath, not by doing trills, etc. It just suddenly appears, usually after the student has mastered breath technique. Once you know how to turn it off and on, then you can choose where and when to use vibrato. You may want to use it on a beautiful ballad, but not so much on a fast-tempo or funky song. Try turning it off and on, going from a straight tone to a vibrato and back again.

how to do it

Learn how to use your breath support properly.

Practice turning your vibrato off and on by feeling the pressure in your abdominal muscles.

Use vibrato for effect in different types of songs and at different places within the song.

rhythm and blues

HISTORY

I believe that, in order to really understand a genre such as R&B, it's important to know its roots. And I believe we all have some knowledge of our beginnings as Americans, when we speak of the shameful trade in African slaves that began in this country in the early seventeenth century and continued into the nineteenth century. But it's necessary to look at slavery, because the pain of this seed planted on our soils grew into part of our American musical heritage. Truly, the roots of many styles of American music stemmed from the blending of African musical styles with the ones brought here by European settlers. As a result, a whole new style of music was created, one that evolved and has become the "backbone" of many styles of American music: spirituals, blues, R&B, gospel, soul, funk, hip-hop, and rock 'n' roll.

The spiritual, one of the first American musical forms, came about as black slaves combined styles and techniques from their African musical heritage with the hymns they were taught in the white churches. "Over time, swinging rhythms, hand clapping, foot stomping, and improvised shouts made black Christian music significantly different from the sounds emanating from white churches."[1]

This new genre came to be known as the Negro spiritual. One of the musical techniques the slaves brought with them and used in the spiritual was the "call-and-response." "Call-and-response forms, in which a lead singer and chorus alternate, are a hallmark of African-American musical traditions."[2] (The call-and-response is still used today in contemporary R&B music). The spiritual gained exposure and became a "creditable sacred folk-music form"[3] when Fisk University, a black college in Nashville, sent its choir, the Fisk Jubilee Singers, to tour the U.S. and Europe.

Another American musical genre that developed after the spiritual is the blues. W.C. Handy, a band leader from the early part of the century, has been described as the "father of the blues." But actually, Handy was not the "father" of the blues; he was a "witness"[4] to the blues when he first heard a poor black musician play a slide guitar and sing with emotional intensity. Handy published the first commercially released blues song, "The Memphis Blues," in 1912, and he is responsible for bringing blues to the mainstream listening (and purchasing) public. One of the musical trademarks of the blues is what is called a "blue note," which is "made by flattening (lowering by a half step) the third, fifth, or seventh positions of a major scale."[5] (We will discuss the blues scale in detail later in the book.)

Rhythm and blues, in its early days, can be defined as the twelve-bar blues form (which we discuss later in the chapter) with dance-oriented rhythms and soulful singing, and was popular with teenagers in the 1940s and '50s. The term "rhythm and blues" was "a name coined in the late 1940s by the record industry; the popular-entertainment magazine *Billboard* proposed it as a substitute for 'race music,' which with the growing social consciousness of the post-war period came to be viewed as offensive."[6] Big bands, or swing bands, which played dance music with strong rhythms and were popular during the 1930s and '40s, were also an important source of rhythm and blues.[7] As musicians had to scale down big bands due to the high costs of maintaining them, smaller-sized "jump" bands were created.

The first rhythm and blues recordings included swing-influenced or "jump" bands and artists such as Louis Jordan, blues crooners like Charles Brown, urban blues artists such as Muddy Waters, and vocal harmony ("doo-wop") groups such as the Dominoes. Many of the singers in these "doo-wop" groups had trained in the black gospel churches, and combined their gospel influence with secular (non-religious) music. Teenagers, both black and white, were attracted to R&B's danceable beats and emotional expressiveness, and the tours of the R&B artists were attended by some of the first racially mixed audiences. The mixture of black church music and popular dance music was an obvious influence on R&B music in the 1960s and on such artists as Aretha Franklin, James Brown, and Ray Charles.[8]

James Brown advanced the R&B art form by abandoning the musical structures and chord changes of '50s R&B and instead focused on a highly rhythmic style, with less emphasis on the harmony of the music. His music can be described as the descendant of African rhythmic musical styles, as well as the predecessor to modern rap music. Aretha Franklin had a gospel music background and was a powerhouse singer in a time where many singers were sweet and sentimental in their vocal delivery. She used call-and-response gospel arrangements on the background vocal parts of her songs, some of which she either wrote or arranged herself.

R&B continues to evolve, from spirituals to the blues, doo-wop, soul, and now to contemporary R&B. I haven't yet even mentioned the huge influence the blues had on jazz and rock 'n' roll (and funk, and hip hop . . .)! That's another book. . . .

So learn from this heritage; it's important to understand and truly grasp the significance of the pain and struggle of black Americans, and how out of this pain, something wonderful and beautiful was created: American music.

LISTENING LIST

I'm going to suggest some artists for you to listen to, and some songs for you to learn. This is just a partial list, since there's too much great music out there to list it all. Find songs and artists on your own and learn to listen, really *listen*. Study and learn!

Blues ('cause you've got to learn the roots)

B.B. King

Koko Taylor

Muddy Waters

Howlin' Wolf

Oldies

Ashford & Simpson

Sam Cooke

Wilson Pickett

Martha Reeves (Martha & the Vandellas)

Smokey Robinson & the Miracles

Diana Ross

Carla Thomas

Jackie Wilson

Betty Wright

Classic R&B and Soul

Boyz II Men

James Brown

Mariah Carey

Ray Charles

Destiny's Child

Aretha Franklin

Marvin Gaye

Al Green

Whitney Houston

Janet Jackson

Michael Jackson

Etta James

Chaka Khan

Gladys Knight

Patti LaBelle

Prince

Otis Redding

Lionel Richie

Tina Turner

Luther Vandross

Stevie Wonder

Contemporary

Christina Aguilera

India.Arie

Babyface

Beyoncé

Mary J. Blige

Brandy

Chris Brown

Keyshia Cole

Drake

Fantasia

Jennifer Hudson

R. Kelly

Alicia Keys

John Legend

Brian McKnight

Monica

Rihanna

Jill Scott

Robin Thicke

Usher

Mixed Genres

Patti Austin

Anita Baker

George Benson

Natalie Cole

Al Jarreau

Corrine Bailey Rae

Sade

Dinah Washington

There are about a million more great artists out there,[9] but I've given you just the tip of the iceberg in terms of getting started. So get started!

SONGS TO LEARN

These songs are considered "standards," meaning they've been around forever, everybody knows them, they've been recorded by a multitude of different artists . . . and you need to learn them. If you know these songs, you probably can "sit in" with any band. I know they may be "oldies" to you, but they are well-known songs that most people know and love. Great songs stay around a long time!

"At Last" (Etta James)

"Chain of Fools" (Aretha Franklin)

"Dr. Feelgood" (Aretha Franklin)

"Georgia" (Ray Charles)

"Hero" (Mariah Carey)

"(I Got You) I Feel Good" (James Brown)

"I Heard It Through the Grapevine" (Marvin Gaye)

"I'll Be There" (Jackson 5, Mariah Carey)

"I'm Every Woman" (Chaka Khan)

"I Will Always Love You" (Whitney Houston)

"Just the Two of Us" (Bill Withers)

"Lady Marmalade" (Patti LaBelle)

"Let's Get It On" (Marvin Gaye)

"Let's Stay Together" (Al Green)

"Mustang Sally" (Wilson Pickett)

"Natural Woman" (Aretha Franklin)

"Power of Love" (Luther Vandross)

"Proud Mary" (Tina Turner)

"Respect" (Aretha Franklin)

"Sittin' on the Dock of the Bay" (Otis Redding)

"Stand By Me" (Ben E. King)

"Summertime" (Everybody—but listen to Fantasia's version)

"Superstar" (Luther Vandross)

"Superstition" (Stevie Wonder)

"Sweet Love" (Anita Baker)

"Sweet Thing" (Chaka Khan)

"Tell Me Something Good" (Chaka Khan)

SCALES, FORMS, AND STYLES

The Blues Scale

The foundation of gospel, R&B, funk, soul, blues, rock 'n' roll (and some country music) is the *blues scale*.

Figure 2.1. The minor pentatonic scale.

The blues scale is the minor pentatonic scale: a five-note (*penta*) minor scale (listen to CD #2, Track #1). The scale in numbers is 1, ♭3, 4, 5, ♭7. There are a million combinations of these five notes. (You can also add the ♭5, in this case a G♭, to create a "blue note," which is a flatted note). The blues scale is the only scale in which the third degree of the scale can be either diatonic (in the scale), flatted, or both. That means you can sing it with either a major third or a minor third, or both. This gives us a world of possibilities!

(Note: some music theorists call the blues scale a six-note scale because they include the ♭5 as a scale degree. We are going to stick to the five-note scale with the ♭5 as a "blue note").[10]

The Blues Form

Study the blues; listen to our blues heroes, the ones who "invented" the blues. Learn how to sing an impromptu blues song. The form for most blues songs is the twelve-bar blues form, which consists of the I, IV, and V chords in the following order:

I chord—4 bars

IV chord—2 bars

I chord—2 bars

V chord—1 bar

IV chord—1 bar

I chord—2 bars

(We use Roman numerals when writing chord symbols. "I" is the 1 chord, "IV" is the 4 chord, and "V" is the 5 chord. We will be discussing music theory in more depth in the next chapter.)

It would look like this on paper:

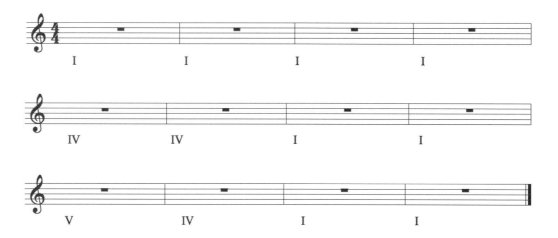

Figure 2.2. The 12-bar blues form.

Learn that form, because you may want to sit in with a band sometime without knowing their songs. So sing a blues! Because of its simplicity musically, most everyone can play a blues progression. So learn a few blues standards so you can go to jam night, sit in with your friend's band, and be prepared to sing something if you get called onstage from the audience. (Some examples of a twelve-bar blues progression are "What I'd Say?" by Ray Charles, "Hound Dog" by Koko Taylor, and "Every Day I Have the Blues" by B.B. King).

OTHER R&B SONG FORMS

Rhythm Changes

In the 1930s, George Gershwin wrote the song "I've Got Rhythm," which became a standard, especially among jazz musicians. It has the chord progression ("changes") of I–vi–ii–V (we write lower-case Roman numerals for minor chords), and this chord progression came to be known as "rhythm changes."[11] Hundreds, even thousands, of other songs have been written with this standard chord progression. One such song is R. Kelly's "When a Woman Loves."

Ice Cream Changes

In the 1950s, doo-wop was a popular vocal style, and its most-used chord progression was I–vi–IV–V, an obvious takeoff of "rhythm changes." Young people were known to hang out in ice cream shops, where doo-wop music was often played on jukeboxes, so this chord progression came to be known as "ice cream changes."[12] There are also hundreds of songs with this chord progression, one of which is "Stand By Me," one of your songs to learn.

Repetitive Chords

Some R&B songs have just a couple of chords that repeat throughout the entire song, with the chorus being built up, or standing out by changes in the melody, or the addition of background singers. (In Alicia Keys' song "Fallin'," the chord progression is simply i-v^7 throughout.)

35

IMPROVISATION

What Is a Riff?

Improvisation is all about changing some elements of a song on the spot. It might be the melody, rhythm, or words, adding "riffs" and emotional expression to make the song "yours." There's a multitude of ways to improvise: you can change the melody just slightly with different notes that fit into the chord (especially useful in the second or third verse or chorus); change the rhythm and alter the "feel" of the song (sing it as syncopated or as a "swing" rather than straight); change the words (add some, replace some); add "riffs" at the ends of phrases or embellishments to existing notes; or add emotional expression (breathiness, whimpers, sighs). Probably the most common forms of improvisation are changing the melody and adding riffs.

A riff or *melisma* is "a vocal passage sung to one syllable."[13] You'll hear a lot of R&B singers adding extra notes to the song, sometimes adding many notes to an individual syllable. Just keep in mind that "riffs" are vocal embellishments, and are not meant to overshadow the melody of the song. Don't overuse them; they should be placed to provide emphasis to the melody, not as a way to show off your vocal acrobatics.

When practicing fast-moving riffs, don't slide all over the place in an effort to get all the notes in. It ends up sounding sloppy. It's better to sing the notes accurately and slowly, and then work up to a faster tempo. Too many young singers try to do all the embellishments they hear famous singers doing, and it just sounds like a mess! Start slowly, singing each note individually; riffs are actually little melody lines within the melody. Each note needs to be sung accurately, not slid to and from. Don't have "slippery" singing! Each note must land squarely on pitch before moving to the next pitch.

Study the greats; just as a beginning guitarist will study great guitarists, so can vocalists. At first you may feel like you're stealing riffs from these greats—just copying them—and at first you are. But then you start to develop your own style, your own unique way of interpreting the song. You *do* need to put your special stamp on the song. Once you've learned the words and melody of the song, you can learn how to create your own version of it.

When Not to Riff

"Silence" in music is crucial; it can be very impactful, even more so than a lot of notes. Remember the importance of the melody and the lyric; we really are messengers, trying to convey the composer's words out into the world. We are the interpreters of the lyric. If we overembellish, then we are really being very selfish, singing just to hear our own voices!

Maybe you've got the most beautiful voice in the world and everyone loves to hear your voice, including yourself. However, notes for notes' sake is not what being an artist is all about. Let the melody and the way you sing it (including any riffing) convey the emotion behind the music. Listen to Aretha Franklin sing "Dr. Feelgood": she takes her time and sings behind the beat, allowing *lots* of space between the phrases. She's not filling every space; on the contrary, she's *creating* space. And that is super effective and the mark of a true artist. She's conveying the emotion behind the lyric and letting the emotion tell the story, not lots of notes.

Call-and-Response

You don't want to riff all the way through a piece; give others a chance to shine. A good technique to use is the call-and-response mentioned earlier. If you're singing a piece that uses backup vocals, sometimes allow the backup part to sing while you rest, then come in when they rest. Listen again to Ray Charles' "What'd I Say" and pay attention to the end section where the backup vocalists come in. Ray says *oh*, then they answer *oh*, and so on. That's call-and-response.

Emotional Expression

Emotional expression can be conveyed by various vocal techniques. Think about a quivering note, a breathy tone, a slide up or down from a note, a whimper or sigh in that note. You think or feel the emotion, and then you have to get your voice to convey that. Ever seen a singer perform what should be a gut-wrenching song with a complete lack of emotion? Boring, right? So emotional expression is imperative in singing; otherwise it's all just mechanical.

A singer who constantly oversings can wear out the listener. It's just too many notes for the notes' sake. Passion and emotional intensity are what differentiate the good singers, even those with great technical abilities, from the great singers. Singing loud and singing a lot of notes does not necessarily make a performance intense, and it certainly doesn't make it *good*. So it's important to find a balance between singing the basic melody with emotional intensity, and singing with riffs that can add to your emotional expression. Sometimes not singing at all and allowing space can be the most powerful expression of the song. Other times, singing in a whisper or a breathy voice can be the most intense way to sing the melody. Just because we are learning about melismas does not mean they should be placed everywhere! Some artists use riffing minimally, just to add an effect here or there, while others embellish every phrase. I guess it's just a matter of taste. But either way, there must be passion behind the notes for the song to be "believable" and powerful.

The difference between amateurs and true artists is in the "delivery" of the song. The average listener wants to hear the melody in the song; we all want to be able to grab onto something we can sing along with. The greatest songs in the world have great melodies. So over-riffing can destroy a perfectly good melody! Even jazz artist Branford Marsalis said, "The most important and the strongest element of music is the melodic content."[14] In a genre known for improvisation, Branford didn't say that singing or playing a kazillion notes was what it's all about; he said it was the *melody*—don't forget that! It's not about how fast you sing riffs, or how many notes you sing; it's about the melody!

The Lyric

If you were speaking the lyrics of a song to your best friend, and this person was sitting directly across the table from you, how would you say them? You wouldn't yell them, or use technical terms or elaborate jargon, so I don't think you would sing them that way, either. In my opinion, the singers who can sing from their heart can convey the deepest emotion. Some singers don't riff at all, and can convey intense passion through their voices. Etta James is one of the founders of R&B, and she didn't do a lot of vocal acrobatics; she just sang the melody with intensity. Listen to "Sunday Kind of Love" or "All I Could Do Was Cry."

I want you to be able to take music to the extremes, both vocally and emotionally, but that doesn't mean you have to do that when you perform the song. Do it in *practice*! Push yourself the box, and do what's uncomfortable. Maybe *under*singing is what is uncomfortable: holding back and just singing the melody. Can you convey the same emotional intensity by just singing the melody without a single embellishment? Too much embellishment is like a hamburger with too much ketchup—or worse, with all ketchup and no meat! Blech!

Singing Riffs

OK, so now that you know when *not* to riff, let's start learning some. We're going to start with the blues scale, which you absolutely must learn; get the notes of the scale in your head, because most of the riffs we're learning are based on these five notes. (I may add a couple of extra notes here or there, but for the most part I'm sticking to the minor pentatonic scale.) Try these out and then make up some of your own.

Examples on the CD

You will hear the basic riff sung very slowly, then sung at tempo with three different versions of the riff to give you an idea of how they can be used. I varied my tone and inflections to show how something really basic can be transformed. There is room after my example, with just the piano track alone, for you to try on your own. The track number corresponds to the same transcribed (written out) number on the music.

Vocal Effects

One way not to sound "stiff" when you sing is to add different effects or inflections to your tone. A simple change of vocal tone, or the addition of different "colors" to your sound, can add a lot of emotional flavor. I added some of these to my examples on the CD. Below is a partial list; there are of course many more to discover and create on your own.

Slide to and from notes (inflections)

Grace notes (quick-moving notes before or in between the notes)

Breathiness

Whimpering

Change of vowels

Growls

"Uh-huh"

Screams

"Filler" words and phrases ("baby," "yeah," "you know," "that's right," "do you know what I'm talking about?")

Placement and tone are also very important to having an authentic R&B sound. Sometimes a little growl in the voice can add a lot. Listen to the differences in your favorite singers' vocal tones. But remember, your voice is your voice! Don't try to be someone you're not; just listen and observe, and if you can use some (not all) of certain effects to enhance your music, then do it. But don't try to have a hard-edged sound if you have a sweet voice. Be proud of your voice and your talent!

Ultimately, I think one of the most important aspects of being an effective R&B singer, or any kind of singer, is to sing with passion! That can't be taught in any book, and even if you learn every riff in this book and a thousand more, that doesn't guarantee you'll be good. You've got to sing with soul and conviction. It has to be believable. You have to convey your emotion through your voice, and the words and melody. The riffs are just the icing on the cake.

Rhythmic Variation

There are so many different variations you can do with just five simple notes. Even if you took just one riff (let's say Example #3), but you changed the rhythm of those five notes while still keeping them in the same order, it would almost be like having another new riff to work with. Or change the *stress* of the notes to create something different. You don't want to sing your riffs "straight"; they've got to groove. Don't be too stiff in your delivery. Try some *syncopation* (putting the stress on the "off" beats). Instead of singing on beat one, try coming in on the "and" of beat one, or even just slightly behind the beat, to give it more variation and "color."

Examples

I have put the riffs down one by one in order in two separate tracks, just to give you an idea of how they work in the context of music. I'm just riffing all the way through, without even adding words or melody. The first set of riffs is in a minor key, performed in this order: 3, 4, 5, 6, 7, 8, 9, 10, 14, 15, 16, 22, 23, 26. The second set of riffs is in a major key, performed in numerical order from 2 to 26. It just shows how the theory of the blues scale (as having either a major third or a minor third) works! I can sing most of the riffs over either major or minor chords. (I've added some variation with the vocal effects, so try to catch those, too!)

Track 27: Minor Riffs	3, 4, 5, 6, 7, 8, 9, 10, 14, 15, 16, 22, 23, 26	
Track 28: Minor Riffs	Sing-Along Track	
Track 29: Major Riffs	2–26	
Track 30: Major Riffs	Sing-Along Track	

Now try it on your own music. It's also great practice to sing along with your favorite artists and try to "dissect" their riffs. Like I said earlier, don't try to do them too fast, or you'll end up with a slippery mess! Take them one by one and practice them slowly, then build up your speed.

how to do it

Study the "greats."

Learn the blues scale, blues form, and blues riffs.

Learn "standards" that you can sing to sit in with a band.

Learn and copy riffs from your favorite singers.

Try your own riffs, and incorporate them into your own songs or standards.

Find your own style; apply what you've learned in your own unique way.

Change the melody slightly, especially on the repeats.

Change the rhythm; add syncopation or "swing it."

Add or replace words.

Add "riffs" at ends of phrases.

Add embellishments to existing notes.

Change the phrasing: come in late, then catch up, or come in early and slow down.

Don't overuse riffs; remember the melody and lyric are the most important parts of the song.

Practice fast-moving riffs slowly at first, then work your way up to a faster tempo.

Don't slide from note to note when singing riffs; practice for accuracy.

Add space, and take your time between phrases.

Be authentic and sing from your heart!

musicianship

Isn't one of the main reasons you started singing that you love music? And if you're really serious about your craft and becoming successful in your field, then it makes sense that you learn as much about it as possible, right? You wouldn't become a lawyer or doctor without first studying all the basics and understanding the ins and outs in those fields, so why would you do that in a music career? Take the time to *learn*! It's important in any field to be the best that you can be!

There's nothing I hate more than ignorant lead singers! I don't know how many singers I've worked with who didn't even know the keys of the songs *they'd been singing for years*! Do you know that the musicians in the band, while they refer to each other as "musicians," refer to singers as—well, "singers"? The point is that they don't consider the singers "musicians," like them. Their terminology says they don't respect us for knowing music and how it works. It says they don't hold us up to the same standards as the other players in the band.

Don't be a dumb chick singer! Know your stuff: if you don't play a chord-involved instrument (piano, guitar, etc.), then learn some *music theory*. Learn about scales, chords, and key signatures. There are plenty of books for sale that teach music theory in depth.

I write my own charts so that I know everyone will be reading from the same version of the song. Also, that way I can check the chart for accuracy rather than waiting for wrong chords to cause a train wreck onstage. Know your stuff! Sure, you can get by without knowing how to read music, just as you can get through life without knowing how to read books; it sure makes life easier if you can read, though, doesn't it? Why limit yourself? Learn to read music; better yet, take up piano or guitar, so you'll really understand how it works!

how to do it

Buy a workbook on music theory for singers, and study!

Take up piano or guitar.

Learn how to read and write charts.

Know the keys to your songs.

Know how to count off the songs.

Check other charts of "cover" tunes for accuracy.

Create books for your band members with all the same charts so everyone is playing the same arrangement.

MUSIC THEORY I

As performers, it's essential that we have a basic understanding of how music works. It gives us more credibility if we know what we're doing, and boosts our self-esteem as performers if we can "take charge." Let's learn the basics of music!

Written musical notes tell us two things: their pitch (how high or low a note is) and their note value or length. Different note lengths combined together create rhythm.

Pitch

Notes are listed alphabetically from A to G. Their pitch ascends, or gets higher, as you go up from A to G, and descends, or gets lower, as you go down from G to A. There are seven notes in the musical alphabet, which repeat up and down the scale. When you go through the entire scale, you are spanning the interval of an octave, which is eight notes. (*Oct* is the word root that indicates "eight.") For example, A, B, C, D, E, F, G, and on to the next A is eight notes.

A   B   C   D   E   F   G   F   E   D   C   B   A

Figure 3.1. The musical alphabet.

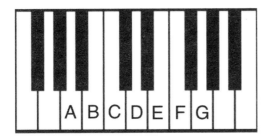

Figure 3.2. The musical alphabet on the keyboard (white notes).

The white notes on a keyboard are A, B, C, D, E, F, and G.

When ascending or descending the keyboard without skipping any notes (playing all the white and black notes in order), these notes are in intervals of "half steps"—the smallest interval or space between notes on a keyboard. Depending on the key of the song, the black notes, written in sharps or flats, would be A♯, C♯, D♯, F♯, and G♯ OR A♭, B♭, D♭, E♭, and G♭.

There are twelve notes in a chromatic scale (a scale consisting of half steps).

C C♯ D D♯ E F F♯ G G♯ A A♯ B C B B♭ A A♭ G G♭ F E E♭ D D♭ C

Figure 3.3. The chromatic scale.

Notes are written on a "staff" to define their pitch. The staff is the five lines and four spaces that the notes are written on. In treble clef (the only clef we'll be working with), the names of the notes on the lines are E, G, B, D, and F. The space notes are F, A, C, and E.

Notes moving up the staff are rising in pitch; notes going down the staff are descending in pitch.

E   G   B   D   F   F   A   C   E

Figure 3.4. The line notes and space notes on the treble clef.

Scales are groups of notes in repeating patterns or sequences. We can use various techniques to help us define pitch, other than their letter names. Since a scale is a repeating pattern, with the same interval relationships no matter what the key, we can either name the notes (A, B, C), sing syllables (Do, Re, Mi), or use numbers (1, 2, 3). Let's use the number system to define our notes for this exercise.

In the key of C, it would be as follows:

C	D	E	F	G	A	B	C
1	2	3	4	5	6	7	1 (or 8)

So we could sing 1, 2, 3, 4, 5, 6, 7, 1, 7, 6, 5, 4, 3, 2, 1 to sing the entire scale up and down. We could repeat this, using the same numbers, beginning with any note on the keyboard.

Figure 3.5. The number system.

Intervals are the measurement of the space between two notes. Going up from C to D is a second, because you are going up from 1 to 2. Going from C to E is a third, C to F is a fourth, C to G is a fifth, C to A is a sixth, and C to B is a seventh.

Figure 3.6. Intervals.

The keyboard is divided into half steps, so we count up or down according to how many half and whole steps are involved. A whole step equals two half steps and is the same as a major second. Thus going from C to D is two half steps, or a whole step.

Note Values and Rhythm

Learn what they look like and their names:

Figure 3.7. Note values.

Notes with flags (♪ = eighth note, ♬ = sixteenth note), when grouped together, are often "barred" together to make them easier to read.

The values of these notes are exactly half of the note preceding them (we're going to use 4/4 time as an example): whole note, 4 counts; half note, 2 counts; quarter note, 1 count; eighth note, ½ count; sixteenth note, ¼ count.

Thus it takes four quarter notes, two half notes, eight eighth notes (hence the name), or sixteen sixteenth notes to equal a whole note. Any combination of these notes can be used to equal the whole note as long as they add up to the correct total value. Example: one quarter, two eighths, and eight sixteenth notes equal one whole note.

Rests have exactly the same value as their corresponding notes. Thus a whole rest would get four beats of rest, etc.

Be able to count your notes properly. Quarter notes are counted "one, two, three, four"; eighth notes are counted "one and two and three and four and"; sixteenth notes are counted "one ee and uh, two ee and uh, three ee and uh, four ee and uh."

Figure 3.8. How to count notes.

The eighth notes above are considered "straight eighths," while "swing" eighth notes are notated in a triplet pattern, with the first two eighth notes tied:

Figure 3.9. Triplets.

Swing eighths are typically found in blues and R&B.

Key Signatures

Figure 3.10. An A major (or F♯ minor) key signature, with three sharps.

Key signatures tell us what note our tonal "center" is and are identified with a letter name. The name of your key corresponds to the note on the keyboard or musical alphabet. The starting note of the scale in that key, or the "root," would be "1" if we used the number system. But key signatures locate our tonal center on the musical staff. The root note, or "1," is not necessarily your starting or ending note, just the note the song is centered around. The "root" chord or "1" chord is written with three notes: the 1, 3, and 5. If you can hum these three notes in your head, you've got your center.

Below is a basic chord (C major chord), which consists of a root (or 1), third, and fifth:

| Chord | Root | 3rd | 5th | Interval of 3rd | Interval of 5th |

Figure 3.11. The elements of a chord.

As a vocalist, it's best to know your key signature and the relation of your starting note to the key. You need to hear the root and key center and then determine the interval of the first pitch. Your musical "anchors" would be the 1 and 5. See if you can hear the root of the chord and sing the 1 and 5 up and down.

49

If you are looking at a piece of music and want to determine the key, there are several formulas you need to memorize:

No sharps or flats = C major
One sharp (F♯) = G major
One flat (B♭) = F major

Sharps are indicated in the key signature in the order of F, C, G, D, A, E, B. Go up one half step from the last sharp to determine the key. (Example: for 2 sharps, F♯ and C♯, the key = D).

Flats are in the order B, E, A, D, G, C, F. The key is the next-to-last flat. (Example: for 2 flats, B♭ and E♭; the key = B♭).

Relative minor keys are keys that have the same key signature as their relative major key, but start on the sixth degree of that major scale. For example, the key of C major has zero sharps and flats. Count up to the sixth degree (in this case A). A minor, with zero sharps and flats, is the relative minor. The major and minor keys have the same key signature.

Time Signatures

Figure 3.12. A 3/4 time signature.

Time signatures define how many beats or counts are in each measure of music. The downbeat of each bar would be count 1. Every measure throughout the entire song will have the same number of beats unless the time signature changes somewhere in the song (this doesn't happen too often). Most songs are in 4/4 time, also called common time, sometimes marked with a "C" at the beginning of a piece of music. Other frequently used time signatures are 3/4 time and 6/8 time. Know how to count these out live onstage. The stress would go on count 1 in 4/4 and 3/4 time. The stress would go on count 1 and count 4 in 6/8 time.

If you are reading a piece of music, the top number signifies how many beats are in each measure. The bottom number tells you what kind of note gets one count. (A 4 stands for a quarter note, a 2 for a half note, and an 8 for an eighth note.) Thus, the following time signatures would be counted:

$\frac{4}{4}$ = four beats per bar, quarter note gets one count

$\frac{3}{4}$ = three beats per bar, quarter note gets one count

$\frac{2}{4}$ = two beats per bar, quarter note gets one count

$\frac{6}{8}$ = six beats per bar, eighth note gets one count

$\frac{2}{2}$ = two beats per bar, half note gets one count

$\frac{12}{8}$ = twelve beats per bar, eighth note gets one count

(12/8 time can be divided into four sets of three notes. Thus you can count it in 4/4 time, with groups of triplets.)

A "pickup" note is a note that starts before beat 1. Pickups are usually on beat 3 or 4 of the previous measure.

Other useful terms to know:

Fermata: holding one note slightly longer than its written value

Rubato: to sing or play in a free style, not in the written meter or time signature of the song

Shuffle beat (or "Swing it"): playing in groups of triplets rather than in equal eighths (see example above)

SIGHT-READING

Sight-reading is not just for classical singers anymore. When major-name artists are recording and looking for backup singers, who do you think they'll hire? The ones who look and sound pretty? Or the ones who look and sound pretty *and* can learn their songs quickly and efficiently? If you can sight-read, you open yourself up to hire-ability! With sight-reading, you can go into a recording session and learn the parts instantaneously. No plunking the notes out one at a time; they'll be right there on the page. You'll learn your parts quickly and show what a great musician you are!

So here are some tips on sight-reading:

You must learn your key signatures, so that you'll know the intervals in the scale. You must know where the half steps and whole steps are. You must also be able to tell if the song is in a major or minor key, so that you can get your tonal center or root note.

how to do it

Learn how to read music; know your key signatures and scales.

Study the music before you start—find similar passages, tap out the rhythm in your head, look for your musical "anchors."

Keep your "anchors" in your head—where is 1, and where is 5?

Memorize several "tricks" to help you learn your intervals. Here are a few to get you started:

> Sing through a major arpeggio to get your "anchors." Ascend 1(root)–3–5–1, descend 5–3–1(root), descend 5, ascend back to 1(root).
>
> "Three Blind Mice" is 3–2–1 in a major scale descending.
>
> "I've Been Working on the Railroad" is several perfect fourths.
>
> Practice thirds with Exercise #3 on the Vocal Warm-Up CD (the Ha Ha Exercise): 1–3–5–3–1. Do it so many times that you can hear those intervals
>
> in your head. Then practice it in minor, so you can hear 1–♭3–5–♭3–1.
>
> Think of 7 as a leading tone back to 1. When singing from 1 up to 7, don't think of a major seventh (hard); think of an octave (easier) with a leading tone to it.

Sum It Up

OK, now you know all of this: how to sing with proper vocal technique, the history of your favorite genre, the great artists and the standard songs. You've also honed your craft by learning the scales and form, and you know how to express yourself creatively and emotionally through vocal effects and riffs. So do you think you've got what it takes to hit the stage? Are you ready, I mean *really* ready? Okay, here we go!

performing

The goal for most singers is to become a professional, earning money and doing what we love for our work! Here are some tips on what to do and how to do it.

WORKING WITH A BAND

Let's face it: If you want to be successful in the music business, you've got to treat it like a business. And if you're going to be the leader of a band, you have to develop good leadership skills. You have to excel at your own craft and set an example for others: getting gigs, making follow-up phone calls, mailing out packages to venues, scheduling auditions, lining up the band, and finding out the details of the gig (what equipment is available at the venue, load-in times, how you're going to get paid). You then need to relay the information to your band in a professional manner (i.e., type it out; don't just yell it in your guitarist's ear between sets at a gig), behave professionally onstage, and take care of your own sound equipment, etc. Whew! That's a lot.

And that's not all! You also have to take charge musically: you must learn how to count in the band, know your keys, take charge of the song by cueing, write charts, and direct the band onstage. You want authority *and* respect, so you have to treat your musicians with respect. Don't be a diva! There's no faster way to lose the respect of the people who are going to be supporting you onstage than to show up late to a gig and then start bossing people around!

What if a band member performs poorly, doesn't come prepared, and makes numerous mistakes? All of these things can and will happen, especially while you're trying out new people, trying to find the right players. Great musicians are more than just great players; they also have to have a professional attitude and be punctual, prepared, and ready to go.

You can pick and choose whom you like, but remember this: never, *never* confront a band member on his or her inadequacies while still at the gig. Call him or her after the gig, or set up a meeting to discuss the issues. The musicians will all respect you more. (If you choose, just never hire him or her again! It's your band, and you're the boss!) Learn to treat your business as any other business, with professionalism. Plus, when you're onstage, you don't want negative energy. The audience can sense friction; they don't need to know what's going on between you and someone else.

And I'm sorry, but I don't know how many "chick singers" I've worked with who show up about five minutes before the band is supposed to play, then start asking why their microphone isn't set up the way they want it, or they don't bring a mic stand, etc. Show up early to a gig, get your stuff prepared in advance, sound check your own mic, etc. If you expect someone else to do those things for you, you're putting your career in someone else's hands. (And a word of caution: treat the sound person with the utmost respect! He or she can make or break you. . . .)

Never try to "upstage" anyone else; when it's the guitarist's time to solo, back off the mic. Don't scat or improvise during someone else's solo; that's called "stepping on someone else's toes," Meanwhile, if there are multiple singers in the band, don't get into a competition with them. Give everyone the chance to shine; you're all on a team and must respect each other.

Don't hog the mic and talk incessantly between songs, either; again, give everyone a chance to do their thing. Remember to respect everyone else onstage; the purpose of you being there is *entertainment*, not self-glorification. You are an instrument in the band, just like the guitarist, drummer, etc. You are all part of the whole unit, so you must work together!

how to do it

Act professionally: call when the club booker says to call; use professional language (don't cuss or even use slang); be polite and respectful, regardless of whether the booker is or not.

Give clear and concise information about the gig to the band members in advance in writing: location, how to load in, payment amount, setup time, downbeat time.

Help load in and set up the equipment. If necessary, bring your own microphone and mic stand. Know at least a little about the "EQ" of the sound (highs, mids, lows, etc.).

Know how to set up your microphone in the PA system and how to check your mic. Don't do a sound check when other musicians are doing theirs; give all band members a chance to hear their own sounds.

Pay the band members in a timely fashion—that means right after the gig! Don't make people wait; it's rude. They did their job; now do yours. It's your band, so it's your reputation on the line. Don't expect others to do for you what you can and should do for yourself.

Never get into a confrontation with another band member at a gig. Set up a meeting after the gig to discuss the situation.

Help break down the equipment; don't sit in the audience while your band sweats loading up gear!

Remember, your reputation can enhance or ruin your chances to work with top pro musicians!

Be on time for rehearsals! Set an example for the band members.

Don't gossip within your own band; you're a business leader, just like in any business. Unless you're all writing songs together and splitting things equally, you are the leader. The worst thing you can do is initiate inner struggle in your team.

Don't badmouth other performers who may be sitting in, or just in the house. You may work with them someday!

You are the star, but don't act like a diva! Keep positive and enthusiastic about the music, the project, and the band. People are attracted to positive energy, so give compliments to your band members; they are your teammates, and you need them on your court.

Don't crosstalk! Two or more people talking on the microphone at once will only confuse the audience.

Keep eye contact with your band members onstage. Don't be oblivious to what's going on around you. Band members usually cue each other with eye contact alone. Keep on your toes and watch what's going on!

Acknowledge your band members, and introduce them at least once during the set. Play at least one song in the set that allows each band member to take a turn for a short solo after you announce his or her name. (Just don't drag it out and turn it into a jam session.)

Don't burn your bridges! If you absolutely must fire someone, keep it positive; don't be hurtful. Just say he or she wasn't exactly what you were looking for, but you appreciate the time and talent put into the project. You may have to use that person again in the future!

GIGGING (PLAYING LIVE SHOWS)

How to Get a Gig

Research and find which venues host your style of music. There's nothing worse than spending the time and money it takes to make your press kit (described in detail later), mailing it off, making follow-up calls . . . and then finding out that they don't use your style of music at their venue. Do your homework. Look in the paper and find out where similar bands are performing. (Better yet, go to those clubs personally and hear what's going on there.)

Call the club during business hours (9:00 to 5:00) and ask who books the entertainment.

Introduce yourself in a professional manner: Give your name, who you represent (your band), and your purpose for calling (getting a gig).

Ask what they would like you to provide to them: a press kit with CD, or an electronic press kit (EPK) from sites such as MySpace, Sonicbids, or ReverbNation.

Get the mailing or e-mail address (depending on what they want you to send).

Ask when is a good time to follow up. If they say, "Give me a couple of weeks," ask, "What time of day is best to reach you?" Club bookers are usually hard to get on the phone in the first place, and harder for follow-up calls. Just be patient. Most of them have multiple responsibilities at the venue, and have hundreds of artists who want to play there. Don't let their unavailability deter you from your goal.

If you're looking for a paid gig (usually doing cover material), you can ask if they pay, and if so, what the pay is. If you're showcasing yourself, you may have to ask if there's a production fee (where you'd have to pay them—yes, it's true!). That production fee covers the fee for the sound person, if the club has a large sound system. Sometimes you have to pay the production fee in advance, and sometimes the club will deduct it from your earnings. There are some clubs that require you to buy tickets for your own show in advance; then you must sell them to your fans. It's called "pay to play."

Follow up at the time the booker said he or she would be available. Reintroduce yourself—remind the booker of who you are and when you sent your press kit, and ask if he or she has had a chance to listen to it. If not, ask again when is a good time to call, and follow up. (This process may continue for weeks, so be patient.) Once you're in and you do a good job at your gig, you can be in forever, so don't blow it by being impatient. And remember, the squeaky wheel gets the grease; if you follow up with persistence, eventually they will listen, because they see how much effort you are making.

Once you get the gig, ask the basics that you'll need to know: Is there a PA system? Is there a sound person to run it? What's the setup (how many microphones, are there monitors, etc.)? What are the hours you'll play, and are you allowed to have a tip jar? How do you get paid at the end of the night—by check or cash? (If it's by check, be prepared to pay your band members from your own checkbook; the venue will usually just write one check to the leader of the band.) Are there food and drink discounts? Do you need to sign a contract (for larger shows—most local club gigs are verbal agreements)?

If there's a contract, review it and return it to the club in a timely manner. If it's a verbal agreement, it's best to check in and confirm the date before you start e-mailing your fans.

Before the Show

The club wants to see numbers; they are a business, and the bottom line is money! No matter how great you are, if there's no one there to see you, you probably won't be asked back. So network! Call and e-mail your friends, fans, and local papers with your show details, update your social networking pages, and carry mini-flyers for chance meetings. In the Press and Publicity and the Network sections later on, we'll talk about how to use these channels to get the best results.

Have a set list printed for every band member. Keep space between songs to a minimum, no more than a few seconds. Within each set, vary the keys, tempos, and styles. Know how many songs you will need to fill the time of your set; time the songs and the in-between time. You can also combine a couple of songs with the same tempo and feel and go right from one into the next without stopping. And have an encore ready; be prepared for success!

Bring *all* phone numbers with you to the gig: the musicians, the promoter, the booker, the agent, everyone! If someone is late, you don't want to get in a panic because you can't locate him or her.

If you're performing outside, where your set lists could blow away, bring tape to tape them down.

Bring extra stuff: batteries, microphone cables, panty hose, makeup. . . . Whatever can go wrong at some point *will*!

At the Show

Act professionally! Don't be hyper and running around crazy and anxious before you've even started!

Wait until the previous band has moved all or most of their equipment off the stage before you start setting up. It can get really confusing with multiple wires and cords onstage. You don't want to misplace any of your equipment, or have it taken accidentally by another band.

Set up the PA system, or meet with the sound person and tell him or her what you need (boom stand or straight stand). (The sound person can be your best friend or worst enemy; treat him or her with respect, and never be bossy!)

Set up the stage with the mic the way you want it.

Check the levels of the microphones and instruments. You'll need a good balance between vocals and the band.

Have an e-mail sign-up sheet available, so that new fans can submit their e-mail addresses. Make sure you announce where it is (at the stage, front table, etc.) so people can find it.

Don't get into arguments with the club booker, promoter, management, or staff. Remember, you're there to perform for your audience. Do business transactions after the show, not before a live performance. It will only spoil your onstage energy.

Don't drink while you perform! Alcohol dries your throat out and makes you say and do stupid things. This is how you want to make your living, right? You wouldn't drink at your day job, so don't drink on your night job. You need to be on your toes, especially if you're handling the business and money at the end of the night!

Have fun! Your love of music and performing is what brought you here. All the lessons in the world can't teach you to just relax and dive in!

If there are problems onstage (sound, equipment failures, etc.), just smile and flow with it! The audience doesn't need to know what's going on onstage.

After the Show

Quickly and efficiently load off the stage. Don't go to the bar or start hanging out with your friends; there may be another band waiting to go on. Unless you have no equipment, get your gear off first! Even if you're the last band of the night, the management doesn't want you hanging out forever.

Get paid (you would hope!) and deal with business transactions at the end of the evening.

After the show is concluded, approach the manager on duty for payment (if you're getting paid). You'll probably have to fill out a W-9 form for tax purposes. Keep records of what the pay is and whom you've paid from your personal funds, so that at tax time you can inform your accountant of your actual income and expenses.

Thank the manager for having you and giving you an opportunity to play. (If you're playing near the end of the night, don't start chitchatting at 2:00 a.m. Usually that manager has lots of work to do in closing up, and wants to do it and go home.)

Follow up in the next few days: ask how things went and if there's another opportunity to play at the venue in the future. Ask when would be a good time to follow up for the next gig.

PRESS AND PUBLICITY

You have to learn to become your own manager and publicist, and it's a lot of work! Posting flyers on curbside poles is long gone. Here are a few tools to help you with publicity:

Get business cards made with your photo on them. Include your web address, phone number, and e-mail address.

Get your own website; this is an invaluable tool in today's marketplace. Every business has a website, and yours should be no different.

Put your web address on your CDs and make it visible at every opportunity. Announce it at your gigs.

Link to other websites similar to yours. It will build more traffic.

Network

Use websites (Facebook, MySpace, etc.) to promote yourself. Post bulletins and event announcements on those sites. Don't just post a notice on your own page and expect people to find their way to your page. You have to bring them there.

Send out e-mails announcing your shows to the local papers. Include the club name, address, phone number, cover charge, what time you start, and a small blurb about yourself and your band in the e-mail. Look in the local entertainment paper; every night the bands are listed, with short descriptions, under the heading of the type of music they play.

Gather your e-mail list: Every time you play, bring a clipboard to collect people's names and e-mail addresses (include a heading for each column, with "Write clearly" at the top). Leave lots of space for them to write their e-mail addresses. People don't always use their best penmanship, and you want to be able to read those hard-earned names the next day! (Another option is to have a contact page on your website where people can subscribe to your list online.)

E-mail to your list at least twice before your show. You don't want to overdo it, but send out a notice about four days before the gig, then again the day before so it's fresh in their minds. Make sure you list all the details of the event: your name; the band name; the club name and address; the time you play (you can fudge this a bit earlier, to make sure they'll all be there for your downbeat); who else is on the bill (maybe they don't know you, but they know the act following you or preceding you); the phone number of the club; the cover charge, if any; and any other pertinent information (CD release party, birthday bash, etc.). Do anything to get them there!

If you can, include a small photo in your e-mail, so they will know who you are for sure. But make sure you size the photo first and send it to yourself as a test before sending it to the list. The worst thing you can do is anger your fans by clogging up their emails with huge, slow-loading photos.

Get on the phone and call your friends! Personal attention is the best way to get people out; they'll feel more important and needed at your show (and less likely to come up with some lame excuse for not being there).

Bring flyers to the club and post them so they are visible at least one week before your gig.

Hand out postcard-sized flyers to people you meet at the coffee shop, record store, etc.

Promote yourself at your gigs! Announce upcoming shows (unless the club doesn't want you to promote other venues), announce your CDs for sale . . . and especially announce your website. Spell it out if necessary (a good reason to have an easy-to-remember domain name), and announce it at the end of every set.

Have a day job that allows you to make enough money to promote your band! All businesses market themselves if they want to be successful, and advertising and marketing cost money.

Have postcards on the tables of the clubs you play that are "self-mailers": that is, already addressed to you, so that all fans have to do to join your mailing list is fill in their contact information and drop the cards in the mailbox (with postage, of course), if they don't fill them out right there at the gig. Have the mailers laid out so they can fill in the blanks.

Say yes to every opportunity; nothing is "beneath you." You never know who may be at the little hole-in-the-wall joint, or charity function, or whatever. Get your voice and your music out there. The best way to promote yourself is to perform!

Press Kits

A press kit should show your professionalism before the club booker has even listened to your CD. It is a representation of who you are. The more professional you are, the more likely you are to get a gig. The press kit should represent every aspect of what you will bring to a venue.

Here's what you'll need to include in your press kit:

Photo: Live stage shots are best. Use something that makes you look like a performer: stylish clothes, attitude in your facial expression. You don't want anything stiff or bland.

Business Card: It should include your name, phone number, e-mail address, and web address (if you have one). A photo card, is best, because it means people are more likely to remember who you are.

Bio: Describe who you are, the style of music you do, your history, special shows you've played (singing the national anthem at your school's big game), anything of interest (reaching the finals of a local singing competition). You want to make yourself sound great, as if you know what you're doing, and show that you're a pro, through and through. You don't want family history, or when you started violin lessons, etc.—unless those are pertinent facts that add to who you are. (If your parents were Johnny and June Carter Cash, then that would add to your credibility. If violin lessons at age five turned you into Alison Krauss, that might be something to put in your bio.)

Venues Played: List all clubs and festivals you've played (with this band). You don't want to list gigs where you were a backup singer for someone else. We're talking about you representing who you are, not what you've done as a hired gun for someone else's project.

Song List (for cover gigs): You want to show that you can do popular, recognizable songs in varying tempos and grooves. The club probably won't want the same groove all night; you want to mix up slow songs and funk songs with medium-tempo rock songs, etc.

CD: For original material, you can put your entire CD in the kit. That's who you are and what you'll be performing.

For cover gigs, you want clips of the best songs you perform. If you're doing an R&B gig, you don't need to put down "Chain of Fools" from start to finish; they know what it sounds like. Just put the highlights on each clip. Vary the songs in tempo and groove, to show the broad picture of what you do. You can also put about one minute of each clip and fade into the next song without interruption, so they'll get the entire gamut of your set. (Don't make the clips too short, though; you definitely want to give them a good representation of what you do. Three twenty-second clips won't give the booker a good enough idea of how great you really are.)

If you don't have a studio recording, you can use a mini-disc to record a live show or rehearsal, and then edit it down. (You'll need some editing software for this.) Just make sure the recording isn't too "grainy" or distorted. If you have to do it over at the next gig or rehearsal, that's still better than sending in something of poor quality.

Reviews: If you've actually received reviews in print, that's valuable! It shows you've played live and actually had someone from the press come out to see you, and that you've been reviewed positively (you'd never want to send in a bad review). If the public has read your review, they'll be more likely to come out and see you play, even if they'd never heard of you before the review. It adds clout to your credibility.

DVD: If you have DVDs, what better way to show what you do on stage than actually showing what you do onstage? Just make sure the audio is of great quality. Bookers want to see and hear what you do, so make sure both the audio and visual are up to par. Put a link to your YouTube page in your press kit so the booker can see all of your videos.

STAGE BASICS

Walk onstage with confidence. Go directly to the microphone and address the audience, either with "hello" or by going immediately into your first song. Don't lose the energy right from the beginning, asking the band what they want to play, etc. Be ready!

Stand center stage. The singer is the featured performer, whether the rest of the band likes it or not! You are there to sing, to communicate to the audience, to be a visual center for the band and stage, and to entertain.

Interact with your band. You want there to be energy onstage and you want the audience to have fun (and have them think you're having fun). Let it be a band experience, not just your experience.

If you are sitting in with a band you haven't rehearsed with, it's your job to count off the song at the tempo that's comfortable for you. (Otherwise, with a band you've worked and rehearsed with, the drummer should count off the song at the rehearsed tempo.)

Smile; look like you're having fun (even if you've had a terrible day). The audience can read your emotions and they will feed off of them. No one wants to watch someone with a foul expression on her face. Smiling projects confidence!

Sing with your eyes open! The eyes are how you communicate facially to the audience. Also, don't wear a hat that covers up your eyes. (If you don't want to look directly at the audience because it makes you nervous, look just over the tops of their heads, at their foreheads, or at the exit sign at the back of the room.)

Learn how to handle the microphone. It's best to unravel the cord from around the mic stand so you can easily take the mic off and on. Get your mouth as close as possible to the microphone. You want the mic to pick up not only your volume, but also your vocal timbre. If it's too far away, your voice will sound breathy and thin, no

65

matter how you project it. (Most performers have their lips actually touching the mic, so you may want to bring your own microphone.) When you hit the loud notes, you must "play" the mic: pull it away, so as to not distort or blow out the sound person's ears, and then get right back onto it for the quieter sounds.

Learn how to dance, even a little. Movement is very important onstage. Stiffness signifies nervousness; take dance lessons if necessary. Then practice in front of the mirror, so you know how you appear. You're the one the audience is watching; entertain them!

Here are some tips for stage movement as it relates to the tempo and feel of the song:

If it's an up-tempo song, move around a bit; go over to the band members and interact with them; get the audience involved (especially if there are repeating choruses at the end of the song); get them to clap or sing along with you; step to the edge of the stage; and, if possible, go out into the audience. Basically, you need to keep the visual energy up, to match the musical energy of the songs.

If it's a slow song, you really want to "sell" the power of the song through the melody and your expression. In a slow or sad song, let the emotion come through your facial expression and hand movements. You could look to the sky or stretch out your arms to make a point in the song. You don't want to just stand there, unmoving and expressionless. Let the words shine through your face, as if you were on TV and the volume was down, yet we could still understand the emotion by just watching you perform. Remember, you're not only a singer, you're a *performer*!

Don't turn your back to the audience (unless you are doing it purposefully, to build the tension for an emotional song). The audience is there to see *you*!

Don't panic if things go wrong onstage; as the saying goes, "Never let them see you sweat!" If someone blows it, just smile and act like nothing happened; it was supposed to be that way. Most of the time the audience won't know, or will just think it's a new, interesting arrangement they've never heard before.

Know what the lyrics in the song are really about; if you're just doing vocal acrobatics and not conveying the true emotion of the song, the audience will read that. They want to see true emotion when you sing!

When the audience applauds, say thank you and bow! Take time to acknowledge their appreciation of you. Don't just run off stage—or worse, don't just stand there!

66

Visualize the audience when you practice singing. It's a known fact that people who visualize their performances do better than those who get up cold turkey. It will also help to relieve stage fright if you've already "been onstage" in your mind. After all, the fear is only in your mind, right?

Talk to the audience between songs; silence between songs can kill the energy. If the guitarist breaks a string and there are a few minutes before the next song, come up with something interesting to say. Sometimes relating a personal story about why you picked a certain song can be interesting. If you're not a good public speaker, then just keep your set tight so there's not a lot of dead time between songs. Also, avoid using foul language onstage. Keep a professional, positive image while you're onstage and in the venue.

No matter what, don't stop the song in the middle or make faces if you mess up. The audience doesn't know it ninety-nine percent of the time; they just go with it, and so should you.

If you do get stage fright, take a few seconds to breathe before you jump into the song. Remember, you have a gift to share with the audience. You are there to give, to share your unique talents and abilities. The audience is not your enemy. If they feel how enthusiastic and happy you are to open up to them, they will appreciate it!

the basics

Here are some pointers on vocal health, musical basics, and stylistic basics.

VOCAL HEALTH

Take voice lessons from a trained professional to learn how to use your voice correctly and effectively. It could save your voice in the long run. Studying with a teacher will help to make sure you're using the proper technique and will give you motivation to practice!

Warm up with scales at least twenty minutes before a performance. Start easy; don't push or start too loud. You want to work your way into full voice (just as a runner does easy stretches before sprinting).

Know your own voice and your limitations. Know your range and where your break point is. Don't push your chest voice too high into head voice. (If you don't know where your break is or your range, ask your voice teacher to write it down for you.)

Drink lots of water, even on non-performance days. Water lubricates the cells and membranes in your body.

If you get the chance, *go to a steam sauna;* that's the only way to directly lubricate your vocal cords. Sprays that you squirt in your throat may help temporarily, but you actually just end up swallowing the fluid. Have you ever gotten even the smallest drop of water in your windpipe and coughed and coughed? Water or any fluid down the larynx won't just stay there; your body will eject it, because it doesn't belong there.

Avoid lots of salt (potato chips, etc), which dries your voice.

Avoid coffee and caffeinated tea and sodas; caffeine also dries your voice.

Avoid alcohol! It not only dries your voice out, there are a million other reasons not to drink while you work.

Avoid milk or cheese, if you find these things create phlegm for you.

Don't eat a big meal before performing. Eat enough to get you through it, and avoid lots of spicy food, or anything that could upset your stomach. (That's the worst thing onstage: having a stomachache and trying to act like you're having fun!)

No smoking! ('Nuff said.)

Don't try to talk over the band; speaking over loud music is worse for your voice than anything else! On the breaks, go outside, so you're not yelling over the house music. (Keep your throat warm if the weather is cold; wear a scarf around your neck.)

Use your monitors! The fastest way to lose your voice is to not use monitors. They are for your aid, just as a guitarist has a guitar amp.

Keep room-temperature (not cold or iced) bottled water onstage (with a lid on it, so it doesn't tip over amongst all the electrical wires).

Don't scream at sporting events and concerts.

Get adequate sleep the night before a performance; a tired body can affect your ability to sing on pitch and may even create a drab tone. Also, if you are tired, it may cause you to put pressure on your throat muscles, rather than using the strength of your breathing muscles.

MUSICAL BASICS

- Know the keys of your songs! Don't get up there and not know what you're doing! Just because a song is on your favorite CD in a certain key, doesn't mean it's your key. It's the same with sheet music; the written key may not necessarily be the best key for you.

- Know your starting note! Rehearse the song enough that you'll automatically hear that note in your head. If you're really unsure, know the degree of the scale you start on, and count up once you hear the "tonic" (the root chord). If you're still really unsure, pluck the note out on the piano or guitar before the song starts, and hum it to yourself all through the introduction.

- Tape yourself, so you'll get comfortable hearing yourself sing and know what you need to work on.

- Learn basic piano or guitar skills. If you can play the chords for the band or your demo producer, you can get the idea of a song across. They will respect you more and you'll be able to accomplish things faster—like getting through rehearsing a new song, or explaining to the demo producer how the song goes.

STYLISTIC BASICS

- Learn how to sing in different styles; it will only help you and strengthen your voice. Different vocal styles use different sets of muscles and different placement. Learn how to get the most out of every style. (Compare gospel to classical to jazz.) You want to be a versatile singer, both technically and stylistically.

- Learn from other singers. Sit down with your favorite vocalists and copy certain phrases over and over until you get them down. Take "riffs" in bits and pieces, slowly at first.

- Create your own style. The more you know about different styles, the more you'll be able to incorporate into your own style. Being unique will get you noticed!

- Don't over-riff!! Stick to the melody, and add "grace notes" to embellish it, not cover it up. (Think of how too much ketchup on a burger only buries the flavor.)

- Don't sing cover tunes note for note from the record. Create your own way of singing them, so your presentation stands out.

- Be proud of your own voice and your own style. Don't try to be somebody you're not. If you have a raspy voice, go with it. Love the voice you were born with!

- Learn how to improvise, and come up with your own "riffs."

conclusion

As you've seen, there are many tools necessary in learning to be successful as a singer, musician, bandleader, and businessperson. It also takes steady practice, diligence, patience, confidence, and persistence to get to where you want to be. It's baby steps, and two steps forward, one step back. There will be successes and failures, excitement and heartbreak, but you do it because you love it, because it's who you are, because you feel it in your soul, and because it makes you feel alive!

Don't give up on your dream, ever! It can be discouraging at times: there's no other business in the world where you can work so hard for so long, and feel so little payback in terms of financial success. In any other business, you'd be earning bonus checks, getting promotions, feeling at ease and working your way up the ladder. The music business is not so cut-and-dried. It can be brutal!

So you've got to have inner strength; don't let something one person says deter you from your dream. There will always be people who don't like what you do—thank goodness we don't all like the exact same music! The world would surely be a boring place. You have to believe in yourself more than anyone else does. How else can you convince them to support you? It's your life and you're the boss, so make the best of it, learn the trade, practice, be professional, and don't give up! You <u>can</u> achieve your goals!

appendix: a guide to the CDs

CD INDEX

CD #1: Vocal Warm-up Exercises

Tracks 1–15: Vocals. Sing along with the teacher. Use this CD until you are comfortable with the scales and can sing them on your own.

Tracks 16–30: Piano Only. Sing the same exercises with no recorded vocals, only piano.

CD #2: R&B Exercises

Track #1: Minor Pentatonic Scale

Tracks #2–26: R&B Riffs

Track #27: Minor Slow Groove

Track #28: Minor Slow Groove Track Only

Track #29: Major Up-tempo Groove

Track #30: Major Up-tempo Groove Track Only

CD #1: VOCAL WARM-UP EXERCISES

Transcription

1. Five-Note Scale

Ah _____

2. Full Scale

Ah _____

3. Abdominal Exercise

Ha   Ha   Ha   Ha   Ha

4. Octave Half-Notes

Ah _____

5. Octave Arpeggios

Ah _____

6. Octave Full Scale

Ah _____

7. Long Vowels Ah-Eh-Ee

Ah _____   Eh _____   Ee _____

8. Long Vowels Ah-Oh-Oo

9. Vowels Combined

10. Legato-Staccato

11. Head Voice Down

12. Italian Vowels

13. Opening Up the Throat

14. Thirds

15. Triplets

Explanations

All of the exercises have been transcribed at the pitches on which they start. All move by half-steps and cover roughly a two-and-a-half-octave range, except for Exercises #7-8, which cover an octave and a third, and #11, which moves down the scale and covers an octave and a sixth.

I recommend starting with Exercises #1, 3, 4, 7–8, 10, and 11. Once you master these basic exercises, you may move on to the extended versions in #2, 5, 6, 9, 12, and 14. You may add the remaining exercises when you feel comfortable with all of the above.

Exercise #1: Five-Note Scale

Keep your jaw dropped in a relaxed manner; think long and narrow, like there was an oval shape in your mouth. Don't force the jaw down; just open it in a relaxed way like when you yawn. You always want as much space as possible between the roof of the mouth and the jaw to create good tone. The more space you have, the fuller and rounder the tone will be.

Try to keep your rib cage expanded. Don't be too tense about it, but don't relax, either. Think "flexible tension," like a big rubber band that is expanded. In order to create "pressure" in your body, there must be space to resist against. If the ribs collapse, there is no way to create pressure.

Exercise #2: Full Scale

Think of the same values as in the five-note scale: open jaw, open ribs. This exercise will require more breath support and also more vocal precision due to the increase in speed of the notes. Be accurate in pitch.

Exercise #3: Abdominal Exercise

Always start with a "Ha," never a glottal stop using the throat muscles. You always want the breath to create the sound, not the force of the muscles in the neck. You'll know if you're doing it right if you feel like you've completed a hundred sit-ups by the end of the exercise! This should only work the abdominals. Remember, the breath passing over the vocal cords creates the sound.

Exercise #4: Octave Half Notes

Think *yawn* in the back of your throat. Visualize the notes as if they are a laser beam moving across the room with determination and a destination in mind. They must have pressure behind them in order to reach their destination. Don't let the notes fade away or splatter or fizzle out; they must be focused and have energy behind them to drive them forward, as if they have a little propeller on the back of them. Long and narrow—like a tractor pushing dirt down a narrow hallway—with even and steady pressure and focus. The last note deserves the same pressure as the first note. Think *up* as you descend; it requires just as much "work" and tension in the body to descend accurately as it does to ascend. Think of hiking up and down a mountain: it's just as hard (if not harder) to get down without slipping as it is to get up. It requires sure footing and a certain pulling back so as to not go headfirst down the hill. Same with singing: pull the tension of the body to keep the notes from slipping down the hill. They must stay on the upper side of the pitch, and not be "too easy" and get flat. Think about the note having continuous energy behind it and moving forward at a steady pace, reaching its destination.

Exercise #5: Octave Arpeggios

Think the same as in Exercise #4, but with more vocal dexterity and precision in pitch when jumping back and forth between notes. You have to get back to exactly the same pitch you began with.

Exercise #6: Octave Full Scale

Same as Exercises #4 and #5, but with quicker-moving notes. Good for vocal dexterity and range.

Exercises #7–8: Long Vowels

These are two parts of one exercise. The purpose of this exercise is to be able to sing the five main vowels, *Ah-Eh-Ee-Oh-Oo,* with a long jaw, creating as much space and resonance in your mouth as possible. Remember, space is the first step in creating good tone. Don't force the jaw open; just open it as in a yawn, nice and relaxed. If you can sing these five vowels with an open shape, then you can sing anything with the same tone and resonance.

Remember, the vowels carry the sound; consonants chop off the sound. So you always want your tone to be consistent and to travel from note to note, vowel to vowel, and word to word. You don't want your tone changing just because the word changes. You wouldn't want to sound nasal just because you had to sing the word "baby" (*baybeeeeee*), would you? This exercise will teach you consistency of tone.

Think of *Ah* as being the mother of all vowels, the one the doctor makes you say to open your mouth as much as possible. The other "Italian" vowels (*Eh, Ee, Oh, Oo*) are offshoots of the *Ah* vowel, but can be sung with as much space. And non-Italian vowels (like the *Uh* in "love," the *Ih* in "it," or the *A* in "cat") have to be modified to the *Ah-Eh-Ee-Oh-Oo* shape. For instance, if you were singing "cat," you wouldn't want that horrible nasal tone in the vowel, so shape *Ah*, but sing "cat." It won't sound like "caht," but like "cat" with a big tone.

Exercise #7:

The first part is *Ah-Eh-Ee*. Hold your hands against your mouth and say *Ah-Eh-Ee*. You feel your tongue rise up and your jaw gradually close. You can say *Ah-Eh-Ee* while holding your jaw, not allowing your mouth to close completely. It will close somewhat, but you don't want the *Ee* to spread wide.

Think long and narrow with the shape of your mouth, especially with the *Ee*. You will have to pucker your lips in order to create the actual *Ee* sound. Try to keep as much space as possible between the roof of the mouth and the jaw while still pronouncing the vowel properly. Practice in front of the mirror, and make sure you can put your finger between your top and bottom teeth in the *Ee* vowel. There must be space there!

Exercise #8:

The second part is *Ah-Oh-Oo*. Hold your hands against your mouth and say *Ah-Oh-Oo*. You feel your lips come closer together for the *Oh* and *Oo*.

It's the same concept as the *Ah-Eh-Ee*, but actually easier because you *can* keep your jaw dropped for the entire exercise. Keep the space between the jaw and roof of your mouth. The lips will be close together on the *Oo*, but there will be space in the back of the throat.

Exercise #9: Vowels Combined

This exercise puts the above exercises together in one long exercise (on one breath). Think *legato* (smooth and connected). The vocal tone should not change as you sing from vowel to vowel. Keep looking in the mirror to make sure you're not chewing with your jaws but are keeping the jaw dropped and long. Hold your jaw with your hands if necessary.

Exercise #10: Legato-Staccato (Alleluia) Exercise

This exercise is over the word "Alleluia." Sing staccato and use the abdominal muscles on the *Oo* part of the word; don't use your throat muscles. It's all in one breath. Three different vowels are used for this exercise; keep the jaw dropped, especially on the *Oo*. This exercise will take you through both chest and head voice. Use the breath on the high *Oo*s, feeling the abdominal muscles pushing the air out. You *don't* want to use your throat muscles on the *Oo*s, just your breath! Let the high notes "float" on the air; they should be high and light, not forced.

Exercise #11: Head Voice Down

This exercise is to help you with the lower range of the head voice. The low head voice tends to be very weak in most singers. You want to be able to sing in both chest voice and head voice in the break area so that you can choose what is best for the song. You don't want to yodel back and forth, but to sing one clear, consistent tone in one register. If you strengthen the lower end of your head voice, it will then be strong enough to sing phrases that cross through that area. You don't want to plunk down into chest voice every time you sing certain notes. You want to have a choice, and with this exercise you will be able to bring your head voice down to a note, rather than pushing up in chest voice.

Take a gasp breath and start on a soft *Oo*, then gradually get louder as you descend the scale. Keep the voice in head voice; don't let it change to chest voice. You may have to feel that you're pulling up the note so it won't fall into the lower register and break. This exercise will strengthen the head register and bridge the gap between chest and head voices, to help them to blend and transition more smoothly between registers.

Exercise #12: Italian Vowels

Italian Vowels are very pure: *Ah-Eh-Ee-Oh-Oo;* it's not like in English, where we have "ugly" vowels ("cat," "it," "love"). Keep the jaw long throughout this exercise. Hold your face with your hands to keep your jaw open if necessary.

Exercise #13: Opening Up the Throat

Feel the center of the tone go from the front of the mouth to the back of the throat. Keep the tone nice and open and centered on the *Ah.*

Exercise #14: Thirds

This is an exercise for vocal dexterity. Make sure your notes are accurate in pitch. You must know the scale diatonically from inside your head. If you were to sing this a cappella, would the pitch be accurate?

Exercise #15: Triplets

Same as Exercise #14, except you must also be accurate in your rhythm. Make sure the triplets are all exactly even, not "swung" or dotted eighths and sixteenths.

CD #2: R&B EXERCISES

Transcription

1. Minor Pentatonic Scale

Wo - oh   Wo - oh   Wo - oh   Wo - oh   Wo - oh   Wo - oh

2.

Hey _____

3.

Oo   Oo _____   Yeah ____

4.

Yeah Yeah _____

5.

Yeah Yeah _____

6.

Yeah Yeah ____

7.

Yeah ____   Yeah ____

8.

Yeah ____   Yeah ____   Yeah ____

9.

Oh   Oh ____   Oh _____

10.

Hey ____   Yeah   Yeah ____

11.

Hey - ey - ey   yeah _

12.

Oh   Oh ____

13.

Hey - ey _____   Yeah _____

14.

Hey _____

15.

16.

17.

18.

84

19.

20.

21.

22.

23.

24.

25.

26.

Explanations

The lyrics printed are simply examples of what you can sing to the riffs; the recordings provide some other options.

Exercise #1: The Minor Pentatonic Scale
Learn it, because most of the riffs on this CD are based on this scale.

Exercises #2–26: R&B Riffs
These are a few of the combinations you can make with just five simple notes. The first example is the riff performed slowly, with space afterwards so you can practice. Then there are three up-tempo versions that follow. I have tried to vary the examples by changing my inflections or vocal tone. Just changing the tone slightly can create a whole different expression. Try them on your own and see if you can change your tone, alter the rhythm slightly, change the emphasis or stress, add a vocal inflection.

Exercise #27: Minor Slow Groove
This is a simple groove (i–iv progression), over which I have sung several of the riffs. The riffs are in this order: 3, 4, 5, 6, 7, 8, 9, 10, 11, 14, 15, 16, 22, 23, and 26. Try to follow along. You can see how many of these riffs work over a minor progression.

Exercise #28: Minor Slow Groove Track Only
This is the same minor groove; try your own riffs!

Exercise #29: Major Up-tempo Groove
This is the same progression (I–IV), but in a major key and more up-tempo. In this case I have done all of the riffs, #2–26. Notice how some work in both major and minor. They are sung in order, so try to follow along.

Exercise #30: Major Up-tempo Groove Track Only
Same groove as above, but now you can try the riffs. Try them in order, then move them around. Finally, make up some of your own! Listen to some of your favorite singers, and see if you can put some of their signature riffs in your groove.

notes

CHAPTER 2

1. Santelli 2003, 14.
2. Starr and Waterman 2007, 9.
3. Santelli 2003, 15.
4. Santelli 2003, 13.
5. Santelli 2003, 16.
6. Hitchcock 1988, 276.
7. Starr and Waterman 2007, 34.
8. Starr and Waterman 2007, 38.
9. Graff, Freedom du Lac, and McFarlin 1998.
10. Levine 1995.
11. Levine 1995.
12. *Wikipedia* 2011.
13. Randel 1978.
14. Marsalis 2011.

glossary

a cappella—To sing without instrumental accompaniment, vocals only.

arpeggio—To sing or play the notes of a chord one after another rather than together, starting with the lowest note first.

blue note—A flatted note, usually the third, fifth, or seventh degree of the scale.

blues form—A twelve-bar song form used in traditional blues, consisting of the I–IV–V chords.

blues scale—The minor pentatonic scale, often with an added flat fifth scale degree.

call-and-response—A technique in which a lead singer alternates with background singers or a choir.

chromatic scale—A scale that contains all twelve pitches within an octave.

diaphragm—A partition of muscles between the chest and the abdomen.

diaphragmatic breathing—Breathing deeply into the diaphragm.

embellishment—Ornamentation (see below).

gig—(slang) A performance, usually with a live band, and usually at a smaller-sized venue, such as a nightclub.

groove—The rhythmic "feel" of the song.

ice cream changes—A I–vi–IV–V progression.

improvisation—Creating or changing part of a song on the spot, including melody, rhythm, and/or lyrics.

inflection—A slight bending of the pitch of a note, usually at the ends of phrases or before notes.

interval—The distance between two pitches.

key signature—The sharps or flats appearing on the staff at the beginning of a piece of music indicating the key (tonal center).

larynx—The physical structure at the upper end of the trachea, which contains the vocal cords.

legato—To sing or play smoothly with all the notes connected.

melisma—Multiple notes sung to one syllable.

minor pentatonic scale—A five-note minor scale.

notation—The method of writing notes down on a sheet of music.

number system—Using numbers, rather than letter names, to identify scale degrees.

ornamentation—Adding variations to individual notes in the melody of a song for decorative purposes.

pharynx—The open area at the back of the throat.

pickup note(s)—Note or notes in an incomplete measure preceding the first measure of a piece.

rhythm changes—A I–vi–ii–V progression.

riff—(slang) Multiple notes sung to one syllable, or additional notes added between phrases.

Roman numeral notation—Using Roman numerals, rather than letter names, to identify chords.

soft palate—The back of the roof of the mouth.

spiritual—An American sacred song originating with eighteenth- and nineteenth-century African Americans, combining African and European musical elements.

staccato—To sing or play notes short and detached.

straight (rock) groove—A drum beat with even eighth notes.

swing groove—A drum beat in a triplet pattern of eighth notes, with the first two eighth notes tied.

syncopation—To sing or play on the weak (off) beats rather than the strong (on) beats.

time signature—The two numbers written at the beginning of a piece. The top number indicates the number of counts per measure; the bottom number indicates what kind of note gets one count (4 stands for quarter note, 2 for half note, 8 for eighth note, etc.).

transcription—To write the notes of a melody out on staff paper.

vocal cords—The pair of vocal folds in the larynx, which produce sound in the voice.

vocalise—Vocal warm-up exercises, usually consisting of scales.

bibliography

Graff, Gary, Josh Freedom du Lac, and Jim McFarlin. 1998. *MusicHound R&B: The Essential Album Guide*. Detroit: Visible Ink Press.

Hitchcock, H. Wiley. 1988. *Music in the United States*. Englewood Cliffs, NJ: Prentice Hall.

Levine, Mark. 1995. *The Jazz Theory Book*. Petaluma, CA: Sher Music Co. Kindle version.

Marsalis, Branford, interview by Chris Kornelis. 2011. "The Problem with Jazz." *Seattle Weekly* (September 14) http://seattleweekly.com/2011-09-14/music /branford-marsalis-the-problem-with-jazz/ (accessed October 9, 2011).

Randel, Don Michael. 1978. *Harvard Concise Dictionary of Music*. Cambridge, MA: The Belknap Press of Harvard University Press.

Santelli, Robert. 2003. "A Century of the Blues." In *The Blues: A Musical Journey.* Ed. Peter Guralnick et al. Preface by Martin Scorsese. New York: HarperCollins.

Starr, Larry, and Christopher Waterman. 2007. *American Popular Music: From Minstrelsy to MP3.* New York: Oxford University Press.

Wikipedia. "50s progression." http://en.wikipedia.org/wiki/50s_progression (accessed October 11, 2011).

index

96

about the author

Terri Brinegar was born in San Antonio, Texas, into a family of bluegrass musicians. She started music lessons with the violin when she was nine years old. She continued playing violin all through high school and was in several community orchestras. She was accepted to North Texas State University on a full academic scholarship, where she began an intense vocal program under the guidance of Virginia Botkin. While at NTSU, she studied opera, music history, theory, and piano. She graduated cum laude with a Bachelor of Music degree in vocal performance, with a minor in music theory.

After graduating from NTSU, Brinegar was accepted to and attended the famed Juilliard School of Music in New York City. However, she decided she wanted to do more than opera, so she moved to Los Angeles and started singing live with local bands: rock 'n' roll, blues, and classic R&B. After many years of performing in L.A., she moved to Nashville, Tennessee, where she worked as a professional vocalist, vocal coach, and songwriter. Brinegar also pursued graduate studies at Middle Tennessee State University with a specialization in jazz vocals. Brinegar is a voting member of the Recording Academy and a BMI songwriter. She has four albums to her credit (three of original compositions, one of classical voice). She currently lives in Orlando, Florida, with her husband, Jim.

For more information, visit her website at http://www.jukejoint.com.